Not Yet, Not Yet
Tomorrow Has Just Begun

KEVIN MOHATT

To contact the author: kevinmohattauthor@gmail.com

Published by Amy Jones Neville, Author

amyjonesneville@gmail.com
&
www.amyjonesneville.com

Library of Congress Control Number: (Print) : 2026905051

ISBN (Print): 979-8-218-91766-1

DEDICATION

For my beautiful wife, Connie.

CONTENTS

ENDORSEMENTS FOR
NOT YET, NOT YET

"Not Yet, Not Yet" is the amazing, true story of a man who died of a "widow maker" cardiac event, and with less than a 1% chance of recovery, was revived and lived to tell his tale of heaven. The journey is well written and it will prompt the reader to consider some of life's most important questions. While Kevin is much healthier today, he had to overcome many setbacks, complications, and challenges that will inspire the reader's faith and encourage one to tenaciously press through life's hard times.

-Vern Braaksma

This book was written for one purpose: to give hope—and it does exactly that.

After surviving a widow-maker heart attack, being clinically dead for several minutes, and then brought back to life, the author shares his extraordinary journey with honesty, humility, and faith. He doesn't shy away from the trials and tribulations that followed, but instead invites us into a story of perseverance, meaning, and spiritual awakening.

This story touched my heart deeply. It reminded me that even in our darkest moments, hope is not lost—and that life can be restored in ways we never expect. I truly believe this book will touch others the same way it touched me, and it's why I feel compelled to share it with you today.

-Carolyn Stone

Not Yet, Not Yet is inspiring, uplifting, and filled with God's message to all of us. After you read this book, you will think about God differently. A must read for Christians around the world. Truly a life altering experience with life after death. We highly recommend this read for anyone seeking reassurance about life after death. These chapters will open your heart and mind as you experience the light of God. It is real!

-Mahlon and Renee Hawk

FOREWORD
By Jake Bollig
Founder of Hyflos

There is a difference between a story and a reckoning:

A story entertains you.
A reckoning rearranges you.

Over the course of my career, I've trained elite performers to control what most people never learn to touch — attention, perception, internal narrative. I am known globally for hyper-visualization training, for teaching individuals how to deliberately enter altered performance states and rewire their response to pressure. My work lives at the intersection of discipline, neurological control, and execution under stress.

When you spend years studying the mechanics of perception, you develop a sensitivity to authenticity. You can tell when someone is manufacturing intensity. You can tell when someone is selling meaning. And you can tell when someone has actually been altered.

When I sat down with Kevin Mohatt in a small coffee shop in Gilbert, Arizona, I wasn't looking to be impressed. I was listening for coherence.

For two hours, he described the backstory and the heart attack that stopped his body — and the awareness that continued beyond it.

He did not dramatize it.
He did not embellish it.
He did not attempt to persuade.
He simply told it.

That restraint told me more than any supernatural claim could.

Before that moment in the hospital, Kevin had already lived a disciplined life. A highly trained martial artist. A man who understood force, control, and consequence. Someone forged in environments where weakness is exposed quickly and decisiveness matters. The man across from me that afternoon was steady.

No chaos.
No grandiosity.
No performance.

Extraordinary experiences are easy to dismiss. Extraordinary composure is not.

What struck me wasn't just what he claimed to have witnessed. It was the structural integrity of the man describing it. His clarity. His restraint. His unwillingness to exaggerate. The absence of ego in a story that could easily inflate one. That is rare.

When we left that meeting, I didn't immediately agree to write this book for him. Not because the story lacked power — but because it carried too much of it. Weight demands precision. And precision demands patience.

So I stepped away.

I went to Sedona alone. I walked the red rocks. I reflected. I prayed. I let the noise settle until the answer became obvious.

This was not my story to write. It was his.

Writing a book like this requires more than surviving death. It requires the discipline to face it again on paper without distortion. It requires the humility to present an extraordinary experience without theatrics. It requires stamina. Kevin has that.

When someone stares death in the face and comes back with clarity, you listen.

Kevin's story is raw, powerful, and deeply human. He doesn't sensationalize what happened. He shares it with honesty and courage.

This book isn't about spectacle.
It's about perspective.
It's about gratitude.

It's about what remains when the illusion of control is stripped away.

I listened carefully. And I walked away changed.

PROLOGUE

I watch the scene below me with great interest. A flurry of activity in traffic, but no cars are moving. Several people in blue are working on a man on the ground. I feel very much like I'm floating in the air above, removed from the chaos below. Above me, a clear blue sky stretches with puffy clouds slowly rolling by. I realize I'm atop a light pole. I return my attention to the busy scene below and notice a red fire engine, number E256, parked, with firefighters grabbing equipment from it. I vaguely realize the man on the ground must be seriously hurt. There is also an ambulance, number M252, in front of my car. My car?

I search the organized chaos, picking out details, trying to understand. I see the man's feet moving with the chest compressions. I see a person in blue with a white envelope. He pulls something from it, discarding it on the ground in his haste, and returns to hovering over the man. His feet continue to move in rhythm with the lifesaving efforts. Fixated by the feet—the familiar shoes—I realize: the man on the ground…is me

CHAPTER 1:
"JUST GO PLAY HOCKEY THEN!"

Valentine's Day 2022 started off like any other Valentine's Day. I got up early and snuck out of the house to buy my wife of 30 years, Connie, her regular dozen roses and a box of chocolates. I had been doing the same thing for as long as I could remember. After three decades of marriage, there are certain things a man had better not forget—and Valentine's Day is one of them. I was on task, as usual.

It was a clear, cool February morning. The grocery store line was mostly men with flowers in hand. I could tell the young husbands who were new to marriage—they had big bunches of flowers, their arms full of balloons and other happy trappings. Connie liked the attention, and I would always make her a nice dinner. This special day was no different in my plans.

I made it home, cut the flowers, and arranged them in a nice big vase for her pseudo-surprise when she got up. The chocolates were ready for her coffee, which I would be making to her specifications. We've always prioritized each other on special days. Normally, we try hard to stay open and available for whatever plans we want to share.

She came down the stairs and smiled at the big bunch of roses. I handed her the coffee, and received a kiss and a quiet "I love you" in return. Connie is consistent in her affection—not overly demonstrative, but always reciprocal. That morning, however, she seemed a little tired. We had been watching the grandsons very regularly, and often it's just more convenient to have the boys overnight and send them off to school. They can be a handful for sure.

I recalled that the boys were picked up late the night before. Corralling two young boys of completely opposite personalities is, at times, challenging. Connie is especially good at this day-to-day management. She would never admit it, but she gets tired. This was our second time around; we have the routine down, and that helps. As a rule, we can read each other closely, should one of us need assistance.

This day, though, something felt off between us. Likely my expectations for more reciprocal affection and attention were not in sync with her energy level. When this happens, we generally go to our corners and are quiet. That day, I remember trying to pull out of her what was bothering her. If she doesn't want to talk, she doesn't want to talk. That day was no different. I remember growing quiet and disappointed that Valentine's Day had started on this tone.

Life had been hectic for sure. Our daughter and the boys lived with us for a few years. She was then able to afford a home of her own and moved out with them. After they moved out, we cared for the grandboys as needed while my daughter worked. They were very much at home with us.

Our daughter has an extremely hard job as a hospice nurse. She would carry a normal schedule, usually, but often—without any notice—she would need to go within an hour as a patient was either dying soon or had just passed away. We are completely committed to helping, and without a second thought, always pitch in. Connie would bear the lion's share of this commitment.

However, our life together had encompassed a whole new dynamic when we were all together. No complaints from me—I have cherished memories most grandparents never have. I thank God for the blessings.

We still do not know what the fight was about to this day. Many can relate to a senseless squabble starting from impatience and escalating to a total breakdown of communication. We agree that we were both failing to communicate effectively, which led to a heated exchange that morning. Things were said that were hurtful in a way that only a very close loved one can hurt you, and we were both disgusted with each other. Such is marriage. Oh, to have had a crystal ball that morning—we would have done things very differently.

Little did either of us know at the time that the harsh words would be regrettable. The hours to come would be spent with her shopping to blow off some steam. I was also looking to vent a bit of frustration. I told her that I was going to go play hockey. She said, "Fine, go play hockey!"

We parted ways for the morning without a kiss or a goodbye. We left each other without saying we loved each other like we have thousands of times before. How could either of us know what was to come? As I have said earlier, what would you say or do differently if given a second chance? Were we too stubborn to let it go and get back to Valentine's Day? Had we missed the opportunity to say one last "I love you"?

Ask yourself right now: Have you missed the last opportunity to say you are sorry? Is it too late to say "I love you"? This is one of the many human conditions we face—irretrievable regret. The forever "would have" or "should have" said it. Now they are gone, and you are left in a cloud of "what if I had done things differently?" Our own inner struggles, the ones we are constantly trying to control, often block our view of what really matters most.

I did not say goodbye to the most beautiful woman in the world—to me. We left each other without a kiss. She went about her morning flustered with me, and I with her. Would Valentine's be different this year? Would we spend it silently, apart from each other in our own worlds? Had our own conditions separated us when we should have been embracing each other and celebrating us together?

CHAPTER 2:
"SEE YA MOSES, GO PART SOME WATER!"

I spent the morning upset. I taped a hockey stick, trying to get my mind off the silence I felt. The morning burned away, and I started to gather my hockey equipment. I wanted to be at the rink early. It was my intention to take my time quietly and set my mind on what I knew would make me feel better.

I arrived at the rink around 11:15 a.m. on Valentine's Day morning. I was greeted with the cold, musty smell of locker room #1. In general, hockey players are sloppy in the locker rooms. I had learned to be neat and tidy, having cleaned many a disgusting locker room while managing ice rinks when I was younger. I found a clean spot in the corner and sat down. I opened my bag to neatly folded jerseys, socks, and other underclothing.

I remember the morning very well. It was typical of any other day getting ready to play. Other guys started to arrive. I was friends or acquaintances with several of them, and we talked among ourselves. The conversation turned to Valentine's Day plans, and I was reminded that my day was not going as I had hoped.

I was almost dressed. Skates go on before I put the upper equipment on. I like to tie my skates tight, so I need to get a good bend over to do it. I had been recovering from Covid-19, and I felt slightly tired while tying them on. I didn't pay much attention and just finished getting dressed. I could hear the Zamboni finishing the resurfacing, and it was about time to hit the ice at noon. Everything was in place and fastened on—time to grab my stick and water bottle.

I am usually the oldest player in the locker room. Most of the guys are 25-40 years old. When we get on the ice, we call it "chirping" when we give each other a hard time. I generally refer to everyone as youngsters or "the children on the other side of the ice." In return, they call me Moses—I was almost sixty years old. We are a friendly group, usually. We are not playing for gold medals.

We start by warming up, skating and shooting pucks at the goalies. You never know who will show up, so we bring a light and dark jersey to pick teams. We warm up for 15 minutes or so and then select the teams. This is when the chirping starts. I remember that day one of the guys said,

"Watch out for Moses, he may be old, but he's a tree stump if you run into him!"

Ha, good one, youngster.

The game is casual but fast-paced. We tend to pass a lot and do our best not to look too silly. Some of the younger players are there to try out for junior teams, so they are exceptionally talented. They slow down for you, but it is still particularly challenging to keep up. As a rule, we play until we get tired, then switch with an extra player sitting on the bench if there are any.

I pace myself, so I don't need to come off too often. When I do come off, I want to be ready for the next player who needs a break. Ice hockey keeps you in motion, and the players just switch as the game continues.

That day, we had two full lines of five players on each side—five players on the ice with five extras on the players' benches. There was plenty of time to rest. We were scheduled to play from noon until 1:30 p.m. I was feeling a little more tired than in a normal game. I still had a bit of a residual cough hanging on from the Covid-19 virus a month and a half earlier. I started to feel short of breath and had to come off the ice a little more than usual. I would catch my breath and go back on when it was my turn.

As the game progressed, I was still playing well. I had several assists to teammates who scored, and I even got a goal myself. We stopped for a break around twenty minutes into the first period. I was still feeling a little short of breath, but nothing unusual. Everyone else was breathing hard and drinking water as well. We switched sides, and I took the faceoff.

Normally, I play defense, which does not require too much fast skating. This time, I started off in the forward center position, which is a bit more challenging. We would switch up occasionally if someone was getting tired. In this case, the other team's center was just super good and wanted to hold back. I might have bitten off more than I could chew. Either way, I was there to play.

The teams were even, which meant you skated hard most of the time. We continued to pass around and make plays. I started to get a bit of a headache as I sat on the bench. I was drinking water, and everything seemed normal for a fast-paced hockey game. Several of my teammates, who were half my age, were just as tired as I was.

We stopped for a few minutes at the end of the second period. We all leaned on the boards and drank water, waiting for the final period. It was close to 1:00 p.m. when the last period started. I was back on defense again. I wanted to pace myself to finish strong. I remember coasting a bit more than I usually do. I cannot recall if I was very active in the game or not.

I came off the ice for a break, and my replacement went out for me. I was sitting on the bench, starting to feel very out of breath. It wasn't unusual at the end of a game to feel my age and the need to pace myself. I was asked to replace an incoming player, so I hopped over the boards and rejoined the game. The game seemed to fly by me.

I found myself at a near dead stop for a few minutes. I felt like I weighed 800 pounds. The game was zooming past me, and I was practically standing still. Something wasn't right. My hands could barely hold onto my stick, and I suddenly felt like I needed to sleep. I was at the far end of the ice. My legs barely supported me, and I could not get a single stride. I just glided slowly past the game moving by me. I was in total slow motion. I felt like I was carrying someone on my back.

I managed to stay upright on my skates as I made it to the bench. My replacement went out, and I just sat there in a daze. The other players didn't seem to notice. Confusion was starting to take over. What was happening? I was certain I was having a recurrence of Covid-19 or something. I needed to go, but I didn't want to quit on my team.

By now, everyone was coming off frequently. I looked up and saw the signal that I was about to go back out. My teammate came up, and all I could do was look at him. He asked if I was good to go. I don't remember what I said, but he said I looked gassed. I told him I felt rough and thought I might need to sit out. There were about ten minutes remaining, and he told me to take off. I said, "See you." He said, "Go part some waters, Moses."

I grabbed my water bottle and headed to the locker room. I sat down and could barely move. It was impossible to even get my jersey off. I was really struggling. I managed to get my upper equipment off and just stared at my skates. I could hardly bend over to even begin untying them. Please God, take them off. I barely remember getting dressed. I was wearing jeans, a green shirt, and tennis shoes.

I was certain I was experiencing a recurrence of Covid-19 symptoms. I just wanted to get home, take a shower, and sleep it off. I remember looking at the clock as I left for the parking lot. It was 1:20 p.m. I put my equipment bag in the trunk and my stick in the back seat. The drive was around five minutes, give or take, to make it home.

I pulled out of the parking lot and headed north for a half mile to Warner Road. There was no traffic to speak of. I turned right and headed east on Warner Road for the remaining mile to our home, just across Higley Road. I felt like I was driving with tunnel vision. It was as if I had one eye open.

I also recall feeling like I was about to run off the road, and I needed to get home immediately. I was feeling very ill and in a strange hurry. I slowed to a stop two cars in front of me. The light was turning yellow. I put my foot on the brake and came to a stop. The last thing I remember was an old custom Ford pickup with a two-tone paint job stopped in front of me. My heart stopped beating right there as I sat in my car, foot on the brake.

CHAPTER 3:
ITS ALL A BLUR FOR NOW

I am relying on a witness named Angel, along with paramedic, police, fire, and emergency reports of the incident, which I retrieved several months later. I spoke to Angel herself, with help from the police department in tracking her down. She said she had pulled up behind me at the red light. While waiting for me to move, she said she watched an entire video her friend had posted online—about 3–4 minutes long. She told me that people started honking at her, and when she looked up, she realized I was still there.

Angel said she saw my seat belt, but nobody was in it. As she sat there, she remembered a strange tap on her shoulder. She got out of her car and found me slumping over my console and stick shift, kneeling under the steering wheel. I had put my car into park. She reported that I was not breathing and had turned purple. I did not have a pulse. When we talked months later, she said she truly felt an angel had guided her to check on the car in front of her. I am certainly thankful she listened.

She said I was too big to move by herself, as I was tangled in my seat belt. She stepped away from the car, waving frantically for someone to stop and help. I spoke to the man who helped save my life about seven months later, in person. He said he had been going the wrong way on Higley Road for some reason—normally, he would have been on the northern end, not the south. He saw Angel looking desperate, thought she was having car trouble since my car door was open and traffic was backing up, and went to help. That's when he found her panicking and me—a man in his car, not breathing, with my heart stopped.

From both of their statements, they were able to get me out onto the street. Angel, who was trained in CPR, started performing compressions as the man who pulled me from the car called 911. The time of the call was recorded in the police report as 1:29 p.m. I had been alone for approximately four to five minutes prior to the call.

Later, when I asked Angel about the experience of performing CPR on a stranger, she said it was one of the most frightening experiences she had ever had. The actual CPR part was surreal. She said she expected bones to break, as they had taught her in class. She remembered hearing a loud crunch, and after that, it was relatively quiet. My face was a deep purple, and foam was coming from my mouth. By the time the first police officer arrived, she was out of breath.

A police officer responded to a call of a man who was unconscious, which was later updated to cardiac arrest. By then, Angel had performed roughly 200 CPR compressions. The policewoman took over and performed about 400 compressions. Another officer arrived and relieved her, performing 600+ compressions.

The fire department arrived on the scene at 1:39 p.m.—ten minutes after the initial call. I later found out that the responding fire department was stationed across the street but had been offline that day for training.

Another station initially responded to the call but then turned around. The paramedics and ambulance from the original station continued to the scene and arrived at the same time as the station across the street. By now, I had spent several minutes in my car and ten minutes on the ground. I had already received over 1,200 chest compressions in the street before the fire department arrived.

The fire department arrived to find my heart in V-fib, or ventricular fibrillation. V-fib is not life-sustaining. I was in serious trouble. My heart needed to return to a normal rhythm, or I would be completely gone. I later learned that a hole was drilled into the head of my humerus bone to facilitate an IV. They attached a 12-lead monitor to track my heart and shock me. According to the report, I was shocked several times. My heart would respond, then fall back into V-fib again.

They placed me in the ambulance for transport, about seven minutes away. Per the paramedic report, I was still unresponsive during the ride to the hospital. The paramedic later told me that as they got close to the hospital, the alarms started going off again, signaling that I needed to be shocked once more. My heart rhythm had returned to ventricular fibrillation. She told me she prayed, turned the AED halfway down, and delivered another shock.

After that shock, I sat straight up and groaned, then laid back down. My heart once again returned to V-fib. I was delivered to the emergency room at 2:00 p.m., according to the receiving report. I was not stable at this time and continued to go in and out of the deadly V-fib rhythm. My condition was extremely critical, and I was quickly moved to the cath lab, where a team was already waiting to perform an angioplasty on my left anterior descending artery, where a blood clot was likely located. Time was especially important.

By all accounts, the procedure to remove the clot and insert two mesh stents was successful. I was immediately intubated and put under heavy sedation. The main procedural questions centered on the amount of damage to my heart—time would tell. Another major concern was the high possibility of an anoxic brain injury from lack of oxygen. Sources say that just prior to being intubated, I was extremely combative and had a hold of someone. I was screaming my wife's name—"Connie, Connie, Connie"—and was strong enough that a couple of people had to hold me down.

At that moment, I was screaming out for Connie. She had just arrived home from shopping and was about to receive the phone call of her life.

CHAPTER 4:
CONNIE IS HOME FROM SHOPPING

Connie and I have had endless discussions about that Valentine's Day. One topic is completely her side of the story. As I said earlier, we had a rough start to the day and left each other without words. I went to play hockey, and she went shopping. For years, all I had to do to find her was look at our bank account—I could predict which store she would visit next.

Connie is a profound shopper and deal finder. We are the current version of hunter/gatherer: I hunt for money, and she gathers things. I would often find items packed away with the tags still on, either because she was deciding on the right moment to present them without me knowing, or because she found a better deal and decided to return it. Either way, the girl can find the deals.

I believe it is a trait passed down from her mother. She was very thrifty, and so was Connie. We built a big two-story home when the kids were in 5th and 6th grade. The purpose was to create a home where the kids could bring their friends, and we could be there to supervise and entertain. Of course, there was a lot of decorating to do, and Connie was gathering quite a bit during that time. I give her credit—she is pretty darn good at it.

In her defense, I really think she likes to go shopping for her own sanity. She can spend hours just browsing. Something about the alone time soothes her soul. I am in total support. We have had many moments when we both needed to go to our separate corners and breathe. The morning of Valentine's Day 2022 was no different. No matter how the steam lets off, we always find each other again at the end of the day.

That day was no different. Connie spent the entire morning shopping and browsing her favorite stores. She was able to gather herself and move on from the tension of the morning. As we later recounted the day, she said she was over it and ready to move on with the special day. The day was about to be special, all right. The symbol of the heart on Valentine's Day was about to take on an entirely new meaning.

She came home at approximately 2:00 p.m. I was still not home yet. She found that odd, as I would normally have been in the shower or taking a nap by then. Around 2:30 p.m., she received a telephone call from a number she didn't recognize. She didn't answer, assuming it was a telemarketer.

A short time later, her phone rang again. This time, the caller ID was a hospital where our son worked. She answered, and a strange man's voice asked if her name was Connie. She said, "Yes." The man identified himself as a cardiologist and explained that he had just finished an operation on her husband. Her initial reaction was to hang up. This had to be a mistake, she thought. I was just playing hockey; this could not be happening.

The doctor assured her it was not a prank. I had suffered a massive cardiac arrest and was in extremely critical condition. She was stunned and, initially, upset with the doctor. How could this be happening? He explained that I was in the intensive care unit, that I had gone through an emergency procedure, and had made it through without complications—but time would tell if I would recover.

Connie has told me many times that she was in total shock. What had just happened? She called our son, who said he would meet her at the hospital. She also called our daughter, who quickly came over to pick her up so they could drive the seven minutes to the hospital. Based on what Connie was told, I was unconscious and intubated with a tube in my throat.

The doctor explained that I had experienced a STEMI, also called a "widow maker." The heart attack had resulted in cardiac arrest—my heart had stopped completely for a substantial period of time. They could not yet know the extent of the damage to my heart and brain. I was sedated to allow my heart and organs to rest. My main left anterior descending artery had been completely blocked by a blood clot.

The clot was what caused my heart to stop. My heart muscle would likely be damaged, though tests would be needed to confirm the extent. The potential for brain damage was high, given the lack of oxygen to my brain during the cardiac arrest. Considering the location and duration of the event, my survival odds were less than one in twenty. The CPR performed by my lifesavers and the rapid transport to the hospital made all the difference.

The doctor explained the angioplasty procedure to Connie. A catheter tube was inserted into my right radial artery and guided into the blocked left anterior descending artery. Using a wire, he pushed through the clot to create an opening in the once-collapsed artery. After clearing the blockage, two stents—cage-like devices—were inserted through the catheter to hold the artery open. From there, I was moved to the ICU, where the doctors went into "wait and see" mode.

I don't pretend to know the true feelings she had when she saw me for the first time. I can only imagine that, having seen her in a similar state during her battle with cancer, it must have been deeply unsettling for her. She doesn't talk about it often, and I usually have to gently pull those emotions out of her. As I said earlier, she is intensely private, even with me.

My son was with her, and I'm certain he was struggling with the scene in front of him as well. He has often shared that experience with his superiors at the fire department where he now works. Ironically, his first job as an EMT was driving the ambulance that transported me to the hospital.

My son also worked in the emergency room at the hospital as an EMT, and everyone knew him. Visiting hours were limited. After Connie sat with me and made several phone calls over the course of a few hours, she went home to tend to our poodle, Gibson. Later that evening, my son was able to sneak her back in.

The doctor decided to take me out of sedation briefly. Connie was there as they slowly brought me around. I had a tube in my throat. This moment is the first vague memory I have of arriving at the hospital, and it lasted less than a minute. I can only recall Connie being right there, close to my face, as I drifted in and out. I remember the suffocating sensation of the tube in my throat.

Connie was saying my name, and I knew it was her. I felt panicked and confused. She told me that I had just suffered a widow maker heart attack and that I was in the ICU. I remember feeling agitated and overwhelmed. Connie asked the doctors to put me back under, as she didn't want me to be upset. Soon after, I was once again sedated.

I have absolutely no memory of anything during that period. I was about to lose several days of my life, but I was still here—very much alive.

She sat with her unconscious husband for several hours before finally returning home to a quiet house, just her and the dog. What she must have been feeling, I will leave to your imagination. The entire experience was a blur for her. Had her life suddenly changed direction? Her human condition had just intensified. Little did she know how much raw strength she would need in the days ahead.

On Tuesday, February 15th, around 7:00 a.m., I was brought out of sedation and the breathing tube was removed. Connie was there early that morning. The doctor came in and spoke with her. Considering what had just occurred, my test results were encouraging. EEG readings indicated that my brain appeared to be okay. Some questions still remained, but all signs pointed to the same conclusion—I now belonged to the one-percent club and would live to tell the story.

Tuesday afternoon, Connie realized she had real estate issues to address for me. She needed to check on any bills that might be due. She had no idea how long I would be in the hospital. She and my daughter were sitting at my desk—a solid, heavy piece of furniture with a large computer screen. Next to the screen was a picture of my mother, who had passed away almost a year earlier, the previous February.

Something mysterious happened. Both Connie and my daughter were simply sitting there, looking at the screen, when the picture of my mother tipped forward, then slowly returned to its resting position—without anyone touching it or bumping the desk. It was as if she were saying, *"I am right here."* They looked at each other in disbelief and asked, "Did you just see what I saw?" Both felt her presence in such a real and chilling way that they were left speechless.

CHAPTER 5:
A PARADE OF DOCTORS AND THEIR STUDENTS

I don't remember much about the morning, and the afternoon is very hazy in my memory. I had visitors—my wife being one of the most constant. She was by my side most of the day and night. I recall my son stopping in, as he was working at the ER that day. I was still trying to make sense of everything, confused about what had just happened.

The nurses were exceptionally friendly, and at times the room was full. Blood tests were being drawn constantly. Wednesday remains mostly a blur—I can only piece together fragments of the day. It felt like I had stepped into the Twilight Zone. My sense of time was fragmented, and I struggled to understand the sequence of events that had brought me there. Connie stayed close, helping fill in the blanks.

Thursday was even more active. More tests were done throughout the day, and blood was drawn repeatedly from me. I was hungry, and thankfully, the food was good. Several nurses visited in the morning, and my cardiologist— the man who had saved my life—came by. He was kind and supportive in a way I had never experienced before. I have come to appreciate this man more than any doctor I have ever known.

The afternoon brought a new wave of activity. Starting around midday, I had several visits from cardiologists and a neurologist, each accompanied by students. The first cardiologist was extremely informative. He explained to his student exactly what had caused my cardiac arrest. I learned an important distinction: a heart attack and cardiac arrest are two very different things. A heart attack occurs when the heart struggles to perform its normal functions. Cardiac arrest, however, is when the heart stops entirely, which is what had happened to me.

My cardiac arrest was the result of the main artery that supplies oxygenated blood to the lower left side of the heart becoming blocked. I was likely experiencing a heart attack at the ice rink when I first started to feel symptoms. As the artery began to become blocked by a clot, the oxygen supply to my heart was being restricted. By the time I put my foot on the brake at the intersection, it had become completely blocked. The result was the widow maker, leading to full cardiac arrest. I had technically died.

Another cardiologist I met had a student with him. This was my first real lesson on the heart, and the student was busy taking notes. He explained that the survival rate with preserved brain function for someone experiencing an ST-elevation myocardial infarction (STEMI) **inside** a hospital is between 10–12%. The percentage for survival with no brain injury when it occurs **outside** of a hospital is less than 5%. However, the amount of time I had been down placed me in the 1% range for survival and brain function. The question was simple: how did I survive?

He noted from the reports that I had received chest compressions and became curious about my lifestyle. I told him I did not smoke or drink. I explained that I ate a good diet, as we had both become very conscious of what we ate after Connie's cancer. He said that for my age, I was in excellent physical condition. I explained that I was a retired fifth-degree black belt and that I had been playing ice hockey when I began to feel symptoms.

I was able to describe the hockey game in detail. I remembered playing vigorously at first, then beginning to feel very heavy. Apparently, this was when the blockage was forming. We will never know if the blood clot developed suddenly that day or built up over time. I did not show signs of artery narrowing or atherosclerosis. The report stated that the clot was anomalous and not typical.

The neurologist, also accompanied by a student, had the same question:

how was I able to carry on a conversation? Based on the ECG recordings, I had been clinically dead, with a V-fib rhythm lasting far longer than what is normally survivable. He explained what happens when the LAD artery becomes blocked. The oxygen necessary to sustain organ life is cut off. The brain depends on that oxygen flow to continue directing the body's functions. This is where the term *widow maker* comes from. No oxygen means goodnight—forever.

So how did my brain survive without apparent injury? In nearly all cases like mine, an anoxic brain injury would have been almost certain. Yet here I was, having a normal conversation just four days later. I again told him about my lifestyle and that I had been playing ice hockey moments before my cardiac arrest. He explained that the CPR I received in the street was the likely answer. Simply put, they did not give up on me. By manually pumping my heart, they circulated the oxygen already in my bloodstream from hockey and delivered it to my brain.

CHAPTER 6:
STEP AWAY FROM THE PATIENT

I was a complete miracle in the eyes of everyone I met. They had never seen a circumstance like mine turn out so positively. My condition was a mystery. My cardiologist had never had a patient survive mostly unscathed from something like this. To be sure, I had just been beaten up pretty badly. My body was sore from the compressions. I was incredibly weak and listless. Mentally, I was foggy—but here I was, alive. I have an angel for sure, someone who stood by my side, urging the men and women saving my life to stay in the fight.

I was moved from the ICU on Friday to a regular room. By Saturday, I was fitted with a Zoll vest designed to monitor my heart and shock me if I developed an irregular rhythm. The device was positioned like a woman's bra. It was connected to a powerful battery carried in a case with a strap around my neck. The metal sensors were placed to read my heart. It was the most nerve-wracking part of my new existence. The device would vibrate first, then sound an alarm, and finally give loud voice instructions to anyone nearby if I were to collapse from another heart rhythm event. Saturday evening, I was released to go home.

Returning home was a blur. An enthusiastic 80-lb poodle greeted me. Gibson was different—he must have smelled the hospital on me. He was soon to be my bed buddy. I took a lot of naps in the months to come. Connie became my caregiver. I was very weak and in significant pain. I had a major issue in the middle of my back and chest. I generally avoid pain medicine. Tylenol barely touched it, so I just slept.

The Zoll vest made sleeping difficult. The cord would wrap around me as I tossed and turned. Sleep came and went. I was lucky to have an adjustable bed. The thought of the monitor going off while I slept kept me awake often. I would roll over, the bra device would move out of place, causing it to vibrate and wake me. I would sit up in a daze, trying to remember how to reset it.

Sunday morning, I woke feeling uneasy, though I don't remember the dream that left me unsettled. I went downstairs and found Connie watching TV with a cup of coffee. It occurred to us that the last time we had been in the same room together, we had just had a fight. Neither of us could recall the subject, nor did we care. The roses were beautiful, and we shared a piece of chocolate together.

The morning was spent talking about the events of the previous week. I had many questions, and I found myself asking some of the same questions repeatedly. Each time Connie reminded me that she had already answered, I became quietly concerned. The neurologist's words echoed in my mind: I am in the 1% club of people who could go through this and live—let alone talk about it. Is something wrong with my brain? Is it too early to tell? This was the very beginning of a prolonged period of mental challenges.

I wanted to return to normal as quickly as possible. My mind was flooded with questions and doubt. What does normal look like now? How has my life changed? I had been spared from death. I really hated this stupid vest. What were the chances it would happen again? How did Connie really feel? What about the two real estate deals that were set to close?

Until then, I wanted to get up and try to be more active. I needed to get out of the house. We decided to start small and just go to the store. We had a few things we needed, and I wanted to make the Valentine's dinner we had both missed. There were a couple of filets and some vegetables waiting for me to cook. Our local grocery store wasn't too far away, so off we went. Connie drove, as I wouldn't be behind the wheel until it was determined I wasn't going to have another issue.

We parked and walked into the store. Connie told me to wait just inside by the strawberries while she went to get a cart. I think she felt I was a bit of a toddler at the time. So there I stood, like a good little boy, doing exactly what I was told.

It's hard for me to admit, but years of firearms training have left me hard of hearing. I am especially hard of hearing in places with a lot of background noise—crowded restaurants and, apparently, grocery stores.

I was standing by the strawberries when I noticed people staring at me. At first, I didn't think much of it, but then I realized several people around me had worried looks on their faces. Connie reached me as I stood there wondering what was going on. She had a terrifying look as she walked up and said, very urgently, "Kevin, your vest is going off!"

That's when I finally heard the battery pack loudly announcing, "Step away from the patient. Stand by. Step away from the patient!"

Oh my God. I was about to be kicked by a mule in the chest in the middle of a grocery store.

Neither of us could get the darn thing to shut off. Connie started unbuttoning my shirt. She was going to rip that bra off me before it shocked me. Now, just picture a couple in their sixties wrestling to get my shirt off in the produce section, only to reveal what looked like a woman's brassiere underneath.

To this day, if I want to send Connie into uncontrollable laughter, all I have to do is say in a robot voice, "Step away from the patient. Stand back. Step away from the patient."

Somehow, we managed to get the vest to abort its shock mission. We made it home without any more drama, and in the process, we broke all the tension. I was hilarious later.

CHAPTER 7:
MEET THE MAN ON THE PHONE

Monday morning, exactly one week after my cardiac arrest, I had my first cardiology appointment. I met the doctor who had initially performed the procedure to remove the blood clot and stabilize me. He has since become my confidant and chief supporter.

Our first meeting focused on the details of my blood clot. He said it was anomalous and not usual for a man my age. Normally, a widow maker occurs due to closure of the main artery from calcium plaque buildup. I had what he called a microscopic hangnail of calcium at the opening of the artery.

That was the extent of my cardiovascular disease. He said my miraculous survival was because my heart was as healthy as a 25-year-old's. He told me it was obvious that I had taken good care of my health and was adamant that we keep it that way.

At the time, my ejection fraction was around 20%. He explained that this was the percentage of my total blood supply being pumped through the lower chamber of my heart with each beat. The normal range is between 60–70%. I had a long way to go.

He put me on several medications. Two were designed to relax my heart while it healed. Two more were to keep my blood from clotting again.

Another was to keep my blood pressure and heart rate lowered. My heart rate is normally around 45, and my blood pressure is typically 95/68.

I complained that I was severely exhausted and asked if this was normal. He explained that I had received many compressions. His example was that if I punched my thigh repeatedly for a long time and then tried to run, I would likely trip and fall. My heart was bruised and needed rest for the same reason. With time, he would know how much damage had been done.

It was now apparent that things had changed. We were both concerned about the potential damage. He assured me there would be damage; just how much, he couldn't yet be sure. I felt the pit in my stomach grow. What did this mean? I had been so healthy.

I asked him why this happened. He wasn't sure. More testing would be needed. So far, all we knew was that I had experienced a profoundly serious cardiac arrest—one that, in his words, was rare to survive under my circumstances. I was extremely lucky to be alive.

I will never forget the straightforward yet caring way he spoke to both of us. My doctor possesses an amazing bedside manner. He is gentle and understanding. I was concerned about my longevity at this point. Admittedly, I felt vulnerable and scared. The shoe was on the other foot now. The memory of listening to a doctor describe to Connie, with uncertainty, what lay ahead for her after a devastating cancer diagnosis was immediately at the forefront of my mind.

I left the office feeling completely devastated. Connie sensed it, I'm sure. She spent the beginning of the ride home doing her best to see the bright side of things. She is the eternal optimist, and I love that about her. She refuses to let me feel sorry for myself. In the challenging times to come, she would be my rock.

I was about to begin a journey filled with fear, pain, uncertainty, and brutal sadness.

The ride home was filled with discussion of what we had just learned. I had far more questions than answers. I felt beat up, exhausted, and confused.

What did this all mean? I had just been told my heart would be damaged forever. Could this happen again? Would I know if it were happening?

My head was absolutely spinning with confusion. I was trying to make heads or tails of the last week. I couldn't believe that I had technically died and yet, here I was. The amount of disbelief I was experiencing was unimaginable. Connie was so soft and patient with me. I was repeating questions as if it were the first time I had asked them. I was struggling with my memory.

At first, Connie was not aware of just how confused I was. Eventually, she came to understand that I had some repair work to go through. At that point, I really did not grasp the extent of what had just happened. I was about to find out what the 1% club was all about. Neither of us truly understood what had occurred as I lay in the street a week earlier. The specific gravity of the event was enormous.

We were almost home now, heading east on Warner Road. The day was sunny and cool. I felt a sense of quiet and solitude as we approached the intersection of Higley Road and Warner. We were on the verge of learning the true meaning of what a miracle it was for us to be together in that moment. Something incredibly powerful was about to happen.

We slowed to a stop at Warner Road and Higley Road, two cars back. It was only a vague memory at first, but this was the exact place I had been the previous week. God was about to completely reveal Himself to both of us. My purpose in life was about to be altered forever. The Holy Spirit was next to speak.

As we sat at the light waiting for it to turn green, I looked at Connie and then saw a light pole on the boulevard outside her window. The very moment I saw the light pole, an incredible electric chill shook my body. I remembered. This is where it happened.

The whole meaning of life after death was about to be revealed in the most amazing way. Little did I know that the electric chill I had just felt would awaken my consciousness. I was about to be thrust into a realm that is still indelibly printed on my soul to this day

CHAPTER 8:
IT HAS TO BE THEM

As we sat at the red light, I was reminded of the nearly two decades I spent training law enforcement and the military to never give up. During training, I constantly reminded them that during critical incidents, help was on the way—just don't give up the fight. Keep fighting. Don't stop. Find a way and stay in the battle.

I noticed a fire department across the street. It must be them. I wanted to thank them for helping me. I was about to meet my lifesavers. I asked Connie to pull into the driveway and park. We both got out and walked up to a side door with a thin vertical window.

I rang the doorbell. A few moments later, a man's face appeared in the window. He opened the door and asked if he could help us. All I did was point to the intersection across the street. The fireman's eyes grew the size of baseballs.

"YOU!!! You were dead!" he shouted.

My reply was straight out of a John Wayne movie. "Not hardly."

His voice went to a fever pitch. "I know dead when I see it—come on in!" He invited Connie and me into the firehouse kitchen, where we were met by his crew. A bunch of kids, really. They were all just looking at me wide-eyed. Some were whispering to each other. I heard one say to another, "That's the widow maker dude!"

The fireman introduced us to his team and an assistant chief.

He motioned for us all to go to the kitchen for a cup of coffee. We gathered around the table as he poured coffee for us. The assistant chief remained standing. Everyone else sat around the table with Connie and me.

The assistant chief said they had just been talking about me. He said they all felt it was impossible that I had made it. I was in terrible shape. He said that I had been without a pulse and without respiration for such an extended period of time that they could not fathom how I was now standing before them, alive.

Then he asked me if I remembered anything while I was gone.

I was watching a movie playing in my mind's eye.

It was a clear blue day with puffy clouds overhead. There was soft sunshine above. The scene unfolded below me and all around me. It was incredibly clear and sharply defined. The colors were vivid. An amazing movie—with no sound.

I started to narrate the movie I was seeing with my eyes closed.

I was attached to the same pole that I had seen through the window, the one that gave me the chill. I was about twenty feet up, looking down on a mass of blue people who were all over and around my body. I knew it was me because I could see my feet moving side to side. There was a fast pace of movement from the people below.

A red fire engine with the number **E256** was behind me, facing west on Warner Road, with the pole I was on standing on the boulevard. I saw firefighters below me. Some were standing still, others moving around the red engine. A large, tackle-box-like piece of equipment sat next to the blue-uniformed people surrounding my body.

A red ambulance with the number **M252** was facing east in front of my car. There were blue-uniformed people near the ambulance. The back doors were open. I could still see my feet moving as the people around me worked.

Across the street, at a local business, several people were gathered in small clusters watching. Others stood on the street corner. A few people were standing in the entryway of the business. I knew the building was a real estate office, as I had passed it often.

I was looking down at the scene and saw a police car facing east on Warner Road, directing traffic. The officer was wearing a colored vest. There was another police car facing south on Higley Road, also directing traffic. People were standing nearby as the blue people were moving about around me.

I opened my eyes as I was describing what was playing in my head. I said, "I also see a white envelope about this big," and I held up my fingers, indicating a size of about four inches by four inches. The look of shock and disbelief spread across their faces. One of the firefighters muttered, "Whaaaaat?"

The fireman said, "Come in here." We all stood up. Connie and I followed him into the garage. Connie looked at me with her eyes wide open. Parked inside the garage was a big red fire engine with **E256** on the side. The fireman walked over to the engine as we were surrounded by his crew and the assistant chief. Connie and I were completely speechless.

He opened the side panel of the engine and said, "How's your shoulder?"

I replied, "My right one is a replacement."

He said, "No—the other one."

I rubbed the point of my rotator cuff and told him it hurt. He reached into his paramedic bag and pulled out a small drill. He squeezed the trigger twice, making a whizzing sound, and said, "It should. I drilled you with this."

I was confused, and he explained. "You were a corpse when we showed up. Your bounce house was flat, dude. I had to get an IV in you so I could shock you and hopefully get you started again. I drill a hole into the bone marrow to access a blood source."

I couldn't possibly imagine what that looked like.

As he continued explaining the intraosseous (IO) device, he pulled out a white envelope—four inches by four inches—just like the one I had described in the kitchen. I asked what it was. He explained that it contained the tubing and needle set used to insert into the hole he drilled and connect it to the IV bag.

I asked what he had done with the envelope after opening it. He said, "I was so busy working on you, I didn't have time for litter laws. I tossed it aside while I was getting you hooked up."

I asked, a little excitedly, "Would I know about this?"

The entire crew stood there shaking their heads. He said quietly, "Kevin, you were gone."

I was in complete disbelief at what was happening. I had just described my entire death scene—down to this small white envelope discarded next to my body. It hit me like a truck. I was dead, and I saw the whole thing. I began crying, completely overcome by the gravity of what had just been seared into my mind.

I closed my eyes once again and recalled the video that still plays in my mind to this day. There it was again, in vivid color. I was on the pole, now looking toward the mountains directly to the south. I saw what appeared to be a storm of light, like a dust storm, moving toward me. The scene below was still busy.

If you live in Arizona long enough, you will experience an incredible phenomenon called a **haboob**—a massive wall of dust that can reach as high as 5,000 feet into the air. It is a literal wall of dirt swept off the dry desert floor by a powerful outflow of wind during monsoon season. You can time its arrival. You'd better put the deck umbrellas down and store them, or they'll end up a couple of blocks away. Many trampolines have simply flown off.

With my eyes closed, I was experiencing what appeared to be a massive haboob of indescribable light. It was approaching rapidly. I could see it coming closer as the light swallowed the scene around me. I could no longer make out the mountains. Suddenly, I was completely engulfed in the most indescribable light. I looked at my hands as they reflected the light, which became more powerful and brilliant by the moment.

I have never been able to find an adjective that can truly explain that light. Imagine trying to describe the color green to someone who has been blind their entire life. It was out of this world. I was completely inside it. At first, it was totally quiet. I was in absolute peace. I had no other thoughts or memories. People have asked me if I saw my life play out—if I revisited my childhood. No, I didn't see my life pass before me. I was in a light so brilliant that I can only begin to describe it as pure and perfect. Nothing else existed—just this pure light.

I was completely unafraid. It felt like what I can only imagine being in the womb must feel like. A womb of light is the best description I can come up with. The light became complete. I recall experiencing a vibration, or perhaps a frequency, that was extremely low at first—like a deep earthquake or distant thunder. It was never an audible sound, just an internal frequency of emotion.

I have no recollection of time in this place. I explained to the firefighters that I was experiencing this majestic light. Time stood still as I remained in that peaceful state. The vibration became very apparent to me. Wherever I was, I told them I wished they could see it with me.

In the final moments of this place, words passed through my body. They were not spoken aloud. No one was talking to me that I could see or touch. It was simply a frequency passing through me—twice—revealing the words, *"Not yet. Not yet."* To this day, just as certain as I was the first time I recalled it to these men and to Connie, it was my mother's voice. My very soul heard her words: *"Not yet. Not yet."*

In the blink of an eye, it was all gone. The light vanished. The scene disappeared. The vibration stopped. The silence ended. The peace was completely shattered. I was now in total darkness.

Terror does not come close to describing my state in that moment. It felt as though I had just pushed off the bottom of a pitch-black lake. I felt like I had suddenly broken the surface, gasping for my first breath. I screamed in a frightening, warrior-like cry three times, "Connie! Connie! Connie!!!"

Where was I? There was no sight or sound. I was completely lost. I desperately called her name, trying to get her to find me. Where was she? Could she hear me?

Immediately, everything went blank. All memory vanished. Complete nothingness.

The firefighters were silent. One had tears in his eyes. The fireman finally looked at me and said that I was a complete miracle. In all his decades as a firefighter, he had never seen—or even heard of—such precise recall from someone who had been clinically dead for so long.

A year later, when I requested the full incident reports, the fire department documented that they had performed an intraosseous infusion (IO) into the head of my humerus bone to access my bone marrow for an IV. Several shocks were administered, with alternating CPR performed throughout. Approximately sixteen minutes had passed from the yellow light, the time I spent in my car, and their arrival at 1:41 p.m., when my heart entered an unstable rhythm called ventricular fibrillation, or V-fib.

Their estimate was that I remained in V-fib for around twenty minutes. How on earth could I even talk or remember anything—let alone describe it in complete detail? People don't survive this. The assistant chief was insistent that I visit the two police officers involved. Just hearing that their fight for my life made a difference would mean something to them. He made it possible for me to meet them the following Monday morning at their briefing.

CHAPTER 9:
THE REALITY OF MY HEALTH SETS IN

It is difficult to describe the psychological and spiritual implications of what has been indelibly plastered on my brain to this day. Every single day that goes by, the moment I close my eyes, I see the video just as clearly as I did that day. Something about seeing that light pole through Connie's driver's side window activated the experience with an electric jolt. It has never left me since.

We left the fire station and went home, just a few blocks away. What had started as a simple thank-you visit turned into something completely different. I kept closing my eyes, and there it was again. At first, I was completely distracted by what was rattling around in my brain. How could this be? Was it accurate? It was so vivid—was my mind playing tricks on me? How could I explain the white envelope? The fireman had said it was impossible that I would know about it.

I think Connie was just as shocked as I was. We talked about the experience, and I found myself feeling confused and curious at the same time. We both began to realize that I was a walking miracle. God had everything to do with this. I was supposed to be going home to take a nap the day of my cardiac arrest. Connie was shopping. I would have died alone, and she would have been the first to find me.

Instead, I died in the most obvious public place imaginable. People were everywhere. Angel was behind me in her car when she felt a strange tap on her shoulder. Why didn't she just drive around me like the others? The man who stopped to help her would later confirm that he was on the wrong side of town for the first time ever that day. The police officers just happened to be in the nearby neighborhood. Too many events lined up with precision and synchronicity.

At the same time, I was experiencing serious brain fog. I still had two escrows to close. There were final negotiations that needed to be completed. Little did I know that these would be the last escrows I would close for quite some time. Money was going to run out. I wasn't sure I was going to be okay. The sense of finality surrounding the damage to my heart terrified me.

And yet, I still carried this incredible vision in my mind's eye. God had saved me. I was completely certain of that. But why me in the first place?

The following day was Tuesday, and I was able to negotiate both transactions successfully. I had to put my real estate hat back on and write two critical documents. It was imperative that my thinking be clear—the legal language I used would affect real lives. It felt as if my brain was being pulled through a mud puddle. Clarity was hard to come by. I could focus for short periods of time, but then I became exhausted. I would push myself to function at full mental capacity, and then I would simply run out of energy.

I was starting to worry about my mental strength. I didn't want to tell anyone that I was afraid my brain might be damaged.

I managed to make it through the documents and sent them off to each party involved. As soon as I hit send, I was overcome with doubt. I kept rechecking myself, convincing myself over and over that I had done everything correctly. I had been writing these documents for twenty-two years. Now it felt like the first time.

The video playing in my brain kept creeping into my thoughts. It became distracting.

Sleeping at night became difficult. I could fall asleep, but my mind never shut off. I had never really struggled with sleep since I started wearing earplugs to bed two decades ago. After retiring from my tactical work with the military and law enforcement, night sounds used to keep me awake. I retired with a serious case of PTSD—post-traumatic stress disorder. Back then, I was so alert I could hear my cat walking into the room. My body lived in a perpetual state of readiness. I could function on just a few hours of sleep.

Nights were brutal in those days. I didn't have typical nightmares, per se, but full-blown violent tactical scenarios that played out in my sleep. They were intense, graphic, and almost always ended in loss of life.

Now here I was again, replaying everything on a loop in my mind. I would often wake in the middle of the night with my eyes still closed, convinced I had died. I would gasp for air, just like the final moments of the vision. Connie experienced it with me. She would notice how restless I was, how fearful I seemed when I woke. As the days dragged on, I grew impatient. Was this ever going to stop?

Wearing the Zoll vest 24/7 became its own kind of grind. I feared it might go off in my sleep without warning. I grew to hate that thing. It was a constant reminder of how fragile I had become. I had retired from a job where I was trained to be violent when necessary. At one point in my life, the amount of internal fight I carried was overwhelming and intense. Now I felt reduced to weakness and frailty.

God had spared me and given me a second chance. Why did it feel like this?

I prayed constantly for answers. I knew God was right there, speaking to me, but I wasn't listening. I was consumed by one challenge after another and felt profoundly alone.

I had never felt so weak and tired in my life. The reality of my condition was settling in. I was on a twice-daily medication regimen. I was taking my blood pressure sometimes every half hour. It became an obsession. My heart rate often sat between 37 and 39 beats per minute—too low. My blood pressure hovered around 89/58—also too low. I used to run around 110/70 with a heart rate near 50. Now I felt like I was barely functioning.

I slept for hours during the day.

Connie was incredible. She kept me stocked with my favorite fruit bars and made sure I was eating. Eventually, I would lose forty-five pounds. My muscles were wasting away. I looked old and frail. My face had sunk in, and my clothes hung off my body.

The chest pain confused me. Was it my heart, or the aftermath of countless chest compressions? My back pain never let up. The sciatica grew worse by the day. The muscles in my legs were shrinking. Electric fire shot down both legs like a lightning-bolt Taser, eventually becoming unbearable.

I refused pain medication. I had seen what it did to people. Over-the-counter medicine didn't touch it. Eventually, I broke down and tried Indica medical marijuana prescribed by my doctor. It helped at night. It allowed me to sleep.

Ironically, I had retired from a job where I contracted for the Joint Counter Narcotics Task Force. And now here I was, standing in line at the pot store. I have to say, it worked very well for the nerve pain shooting down my legs. Don't be fooled, though—there's a tradeoff. It made me feel dull and sleepy. At the time, I suppose it helped ease my anxiety. My doctor had me on a micro-dose, so I was comfortable with that.

Even with some relief, I was falling into a funk. I prayed every day and night, asking God to help me through this. My prayers felt unanswered. I didn't understand why I felt so burdened after surviving such a massive miracle. No doubt, I wasn't supposed to be alive, and I should have been rejoicing. Yet here I was, trapped in stress and relentless pain. I was spiraling downward and didn't know how to stop it.

I felt like I was upside down in a five-foot hole. No matter what I tried, the pain in my back and legs wouldn't ease. I was terrified I was losing my mind. Everything felt foggy and just out of reach. I couldn't focus or concentrate for long. Names escaped me, even when the faces were familiar. As a real estate agent, not remembering number sequences was terrifying.

I had ninety days to go before the vest would come off. I set a goal: I would return to the ice rink. My instincts to fight were kicking in. If anything, my mental health was at stake. I kept seeing my cardiologist regularly. He was patient and attentive. I told him about my goal to get back on the ice. He was supportive, but cautious—he wanted to wait and see.

The next several months were filled with checkups and testing. My first ultrasound measured the damage to my heart. The results were sobering. My doctor explained that I had substantial damage to the left anterior side of my heart, supplied by the Left Anterior Descending artery. He always tried to encourage me by pointing out how healthy the rest of my heart was.

CHAPTER 10:
HAS ANYONE EVER DONE CPR?

For anyone reading this who has ever had to perform CPR, you know fatigue is very real. I was a certified CPR instructor throughout my years teaching law enforcement and martial arts. I first became certified in the late 1980s and taught people from all walks of life. Watching students test on the mannequin, you could see just how serious it was for them. Many had small children. Others worked in health care. Often, participants shared stories about close family members who were cardiac-compromised.

The motivations of my students were mixed. Some were worried about loved ones. Others needed certification for their jobs. My message was always the same: perform CPR for two minutes and then seek help. A person is very unlikely to revive from chest compressions alone without professional intervention. In my case, I was surprised by how long my first responders continued CPR. That is a very long time to stare at a lifeless body, hoping help arrives soon. I am deeply thankful they did. They saved my brain.

During classes, I would show a video explaining the heart and its primary functions. Along with it, I shared my own experience performing CPR on an elderly man I came upon in the dead of summer in 1989. I was playing golf on a sunny afternoon, nearly 105 degrees. The gentleman had collapsed and expired, leaning against the only lonely palm tree on the entire course. He clearly had no business being out in that kind of heat. I performed compressions on him to no avail.

Hearing my own voice, I scooped him up into a firefighter carry and jogged the entire distance from the far end of the course. As I ran straight down the 16th fairway, I could hear fire trucks faintly in the background. Someone had seen me carrying the old man. A fire truck eventually rolled straight down the middle of the golf course toward me. I was exhausted and out of breath. He probably weighed about 150 pounds, wrapped around my shoulders like a sweater. It was brutally hot, and my mouth was completely dry. The firefighters jumped out and took him from me.

Unfortunately, the old gentleman had just played his last round of golf.

I recount this experience to share something important: once you hear the ribcage crack beneath the weight of your body as you deliberately force the sternum down to make the heart pump, you will never forget the face of the person—or the horrific sound it makes. Nevertheless, do not give up. Do everything you can to stay in the fight. Their life depends on it.

I taught my students that if the person was a stranger, perform compressions as if their family were standing right beside you, cheering you on. Just keep going.

A couple of weeks after meeting my firefighter lifesavers, it was arranged for me to attend a 5:00 a.m. police briefing. I had not yet met the two police officers who responded and performed most of the CPR. I was intent on thanking the first responders who simply kept going until help arrived. In my previous career as a trainer, my core message to every officer I taught was simple: never give up the fight. At all costs, keep fighting with everything you have. Help will come—just stay in the fight.

I was about to meet my two favorite police officers. These men were real-life heroes.

Connie drove me, as she had been driving me everywhere. A 5:00 a.m. briefing was no small ask—especially that early unless it involved a hockey game for the grandsons. I had attended many police briefings over the years. They were typically mundane and procedural. Often, a recent incident was reviewed by the watch commander, followed by a rundown of the local activity hot sheet—things officers needed to be mindful of as they headed out onto the streets.

We arrived at the precinct and were greeted by a friendly lieutenant who seemed genuinely pleased to meet us both. We spoke for a few minutes. I was about to become the talk of the department. He had intentionally kept it quiet that I would be attending the morning briefing. He then motioned for us to follow him into the briefing room.

Connie and I walked into a room of about thirty police officers. I could tell she was uncomfortable. Every eye in the room was on us. Having been the recipient of those stares in the past, it brought back memories of a time when I felt as if I were being sized up with criticism written across their faces. *Who are these two people wasting my morning?* seemed to fill the air. The watch commander was already speaking, explaining events from the night before.

The lieutenant interrupted him and took the floor. Everyone visibly perked up. When the man in charge speaks, people listen.

"How many of you here have performed CPR?" he asked. Much to our collective surprise, every hand in the room went up.

"Keep your hand up if they survived." Every single hand went down.

I felt my throat tighten. I was on the verge of crying in front of a room full of police officers.

The lieutenant introduced me and briefly explained why I was there that morning. Having attended dozens of briefings in my past life, it felt natural to observe them as closely as they were observing me. I still didn't know who my lifesavers were—until I did. I recalled my vision and suddenly spotted them. They were whispering to each other, subtly pointing in my direction, studying me with intent.

"You two," I said, pointing directly at them. "Thank you."

The look on their faces was solid gold. They had just seen a ghost. The man whose chest they had crushed for ten solid minutes was standing right in front of them. They were in complete shock—not only that I was alive and breathing, but that I could identify them when I had been clinically dead while they were working on me.

The room erupted in applause. I was *that* guy—the "Widow Maker Dude." I later learned I had become something of a legend among the officers.

They both came forward, and we hugged through tears. Even now, writing this, it brings tears to my eyes. That moment changed their lives forever, just as they had changed mine. How was this possible? You don't perform CPR on someone for ten minutes who is alive. I was gone—and yet there I was, holding them both.

I told my story to the room.

The disbelief on their faces said everything. They had witnessed a complete and total miracle. The reality of God's presence seemed to sweep through the room. These officers understood exactly what it meant to push on a corpse for as long as it takes for help to arrive too late. And yet here I was, describing the entire scene in full technicolor—right down to the small white envelope I had mentioned weeks earlier.

To this day, if I tell a local officer that I'm the "Widow Maker Dude," they know exactly where they were when they heard about me. I am forever indebted to the men and women who refused to give up.

I believe God's hand was on those two officers the entire time they pressed on my chest. Without their perseverance, my purpose would have ended right there in the street. But it was not to be. They were two pieces in a much larger orchestra.

After the briefing, I spoke with both officers privately. We were all in tears. We hugged and agreed that God had been present that day. The music was written in heaven, and the Maestro had only just begun arranging the symphony He had planned for me. I simply needed to learn how to listen—and trust the divine plan.

A couple of days later, the police department called and asked if I would be comfortable with a local TV station interviewing me. I had become a story that would highlight the department, and I was more than happy to accommodate whatever the story would become. Newspapers also reached out, wanting to interview me about the miracle.

I decided to write a letter to the mayor, the chief of police, and the fire chief. In the first section, I described in detail the lengths my lifesavers had gone to in order to keep me in the fight for my life. I asked the mayor to recognize each member of the team with a commendation or award of some kind to honor their heroism.

In the second section, I insisted that each of the three city leaders go outside, kneel on hard asphalt, and perform 1,200-plus repetitions of *anything*, and then explain why each squad car was not equipped with an automated external defibrillator (AED). An AED applied to a person whose heart has fallen into an unsustainable rhythm can often return it to a sustainable one, at least buying time until professionals arrive. I don't know whether an AED would have worked in my case, but the device has saved thousands of lives, and I wanted that protection for the officers serving my community.

Around that time, I met a former Special Weapons and Tactics (SWAT) officer who had suffered a cardiac arrest the year prior. He could no longer participate in special teams and had begun spearheading a push for AEDs. Nearly a year later, the city council voted to accept a one-million-dollar grant, and through our collective efforts, I am proud to say that every squad car in our city is now outfitted with a trained officer and an AED.

God provides when we ask and have faith in His will, not ours. God delivers because He promised He would. Even as I witnessed His promises being fulfilled, I was about to experience more evidence of His faithfulness.

***He who calls you is faithful, who also will do it"* —1 Thessalonians 5:24**

Shortly after the television interview, a phone call came from New York City. She introduced herself as Anna. Someone had sent her the video of my interview. Anna was a ghostwriter—someone who helps would-be authors tell their stories. I later learned she had been involved with dozens of New

York Times bestsellers. As a ghostwriter, she honored her pledge of anonymity; the books bore the names of others, not hers.

Anna asked if she could fly out to meet me. She wanted to author my book. We met for several hours at my favorite coffee shop, and by the end of that meeting, we both committed to completing the project. She was certain the world wanted to hear my story.

Little did either of us know where this miracle would actually lead. I wasn't quite ready. I felt I still had a long way to go before reaching the end of my journey. God had much more in store. I was about to find out what He had in mind, and it would be a roller-coaster ride of epic proportions—the kind where you just have to buckle up, Buttercup.

We discussed how to draft a book, and Anna was instrumental in cheering me along. Her husband had recently suffered a stroke, and she found herself in the same place as Connie—a caregiver. Her once strong and capable husband was now weak and dependent on her. As time went on, I kept Anna updated on my progress. She offered constant encouragement.

Meanwhile, I was searching for the end of the story that never seemed to come. She assured me it would—and told me to just keep writing.

CHAPTER 11:
THE LOOK YOU GET WHEN THEY THINK YOU ARE ABOUT TO DIE

As the days turned to weeks, I found myself heading into cardio-rehab. My number one concern was returning to my active self. More than anything, I wanted to get back on the ice and play hockey. Part of it was simply love for the game. The other part was fear—fear that if I couldn't shake this new weakness, I might die again. That fear crept up on me often.

It's a real fear, one that thousands of survivors like me experience. Yes, we are alive, but will we stay that way? I felt like I had a ticking time bomb in my chest. My cardiologist suggested attending cardio-rehab twice a week for two months. For now, any activity I did needed supervision. My confidence in my health was eroding day by day. My chest still hurt, and every little pang sent me reeling.

Before rehab, I needed a referral from a primary doctor for insurance. Since I didn't have one, I picked the first clinic that would take me. I found myself in a walk-in clinic filled with the usual checkup crowd. Three short weeks ago, I had been dead in the street. "Wait until they get a load of me," I thought.

Connie was always with me during these visits. When we were called back, the exam room was small, like all the others, with a couple of chairs, an exam table, and posters warning of various ailments. The young technician greeted me first, weighing me and asking the standard questions.

She began taking my blood pressure and heart rate. She took it twice. I should have known what she was thinking. My blood pressure was 86/59, and my heart rate was 36. A worried look crossed her face, and she asked me to sit while she called the doctor.

Within two minutes, he arrived. Calm, composed, he crossed his legs and asked how I was feeling. I said I felt okay. He shook his head and said, "Let's talk about the bradycardia and low blood pressure that scared the heck out of my assistant." She was standing by, ready to call 911. I chuckled. "I had a widow maker three weeks ago and was gone for about twenty minutes in the street." He smiled, "That explains it. Welcome back." He immediately drew some blood for tests. He was the second coolest doctor I've ever had.

This man became genuinely invested in my health. He agreed wholeheartedly with the cardio-rehab referral. I knew he was like me when I noticed the imprint of his concealed pistol beneath his suit jacket during the blood-test visit. We talked at length about my physical history and my previous career as a law-enforcement firearms instructor.

As we spoke, I said, "Smith & Wesson .38, five-shot." He looked surprised. "Excuse me?" I pointed to his side and smiled. He smiled back and nodded. We became fast friends. I was disappointed when, eight months later, he left the clinic and returned to the hospital. His replacement was a nurse practitioner with the bedside manner of an IRS tax auditor.

I started rehab the day after that visit. The ladies at the hospital's rehab unit were great. I was the first patient they had ever had with my story. They were a little perplexed by my low blood pressure and treated me like a mother hen. Every visit, I would get hooked up to the monitors and start on the treadmill for about an hour. They wouldn't let me go very fast, which was a little frustrating.

I figured out that the rehab staff had been instructed to keep me at a very low pace by my doctors. My heart rate would rarely get into the 90s and often fell into the 40s during exertion. I never felt distress—just tired. The low heart rate was essentially a side effect of a medication I was taking to lower my blood pressure. In hindsight, I was on it needlessly, as my overall cardiovascular fitness already kept my blood pressure low. My heart was an anomaly to everyone who examined me. I was not a typical STEMI (ST-elevation myocardial infarction; widow maker) patient. Normally, several contributing factors—high blood pressure, diabetes, other health issues—would have played a role in a cardiac arrest. In my case, the only possible culprit seemed to be the Covid-19 vaccination I had reluctantly received for Connie's sake during her cancer battle.

I approached every aspect of my recovery proactively. I wanted, more than anything, to feel normal again. I would soon learn that my old normal and my new normal were entirely different. Things I had once taken for granted became priorities. We had always tried to eat well, but now we paid even closer attention to how we fueled our bodies. I also relied on several naps each day. Stress, already part of being a real estate agent, was building, and I found myself increasingly apprehensive.

Living with a device designed to shock me at a moment's notice was a daily stress point. It would occasionally start its warning sequence for no reason. Driving was out of the question, which cut into my independence—a core part of my personality. Changes were inevitable, but they were happening fast, and I felt my old self slipping away.

Connie knew I was frustrated, but she didn't realize how worried I was about my memory. I remember a day when I was looking right at her, having a conversation, and for the briefest moment her name escaped me. My heart skipped a beat, and a sick feeling settled in my stomach. I would often try to recall a name while picturing the person in my mind's eye. Sometimes I knew exactly what I wanted to say, but the words wouldn't come. Early on, these memory issues were constant, and I was painfully aware of them.

Because both of my parents had passed from dementia and Alzheimer's, I became obsessed with the idea that my brain was damaged. I felt I was far too young to endure that kind of misery. The worry compounded itself, and I silently prayed, "Dear God, take this away from me."

I have since spoken with many others who experienced memory issues after cardiac arrest. I learned I wasn't alone. I shared my concerns with my cardiologist, who was very understanding. He reminded me that I had been through an extraordinarily traumatic event. Both physical and emotional symptoms were expected—and I was experiencing a big dose of both. I had to ask myself: what could I do to ease some of my fears?

I was already attending cardio-rehab and proving to myself that moderate exercise wouldn't kill me. But what about my brain? How would I know if it was truly damaged or just recovering? It was decided that I would undergo a complete neurological workup, including cognitive tests and scans.

I feel this part was crucial to my recovery because it allowed me to face reality. I had been confronting the consequences of my death every day. It was important to separate the facts of recovery from the fears I created in my mind. I took my first written cognitive test, and it came back normal. Next came an EEG and MRI.

The day of the scans arrived. I was hooked up to the EEG and told to relax and shut my eyes. As soon as I did, it was there again—the entire scene of my death playing vividly in my mind. Every time I closed my eyes, the memory returned, just as intense as before. Even with the bright flashing lights of the test penetrating my eyelids, the scene remained the same. I was engulfed in that indescribable light and could sense the same vibration or frequency. Even now, all I have to do is close my eyes, and I can recall the incredible peace of that light.

The part of my ethereal journey where I was enveloped in light was magnified by the random test lights. The video in my mind felt more powerful than ever. The vividness of my recall left me emotional throughout the test. I wasn't sure what to make of my feelings, but they were real and intense.

The next test was a functional MRI. I had undergone many of these before, so I was used to the claustrophobic feeling of lying still while the machine clanked and buzzed. I relaxed and shut my eyes. Once again, the pole and the entire scene were before me. As I approached the part where I was engulfed by the light, I lost myself completely in the memory. The sounds of the machine faded into nothing—there were no sounds, only the scene moving from the trucks to the wall of light, and then nothing but the light and peace.

I felt that same incredible peace again. Words still cannot describe it. The sense of total calm felt like pure love—the kind of love that brings comfort, serenity, and complete security. Just as the words *"Not yet. Not yet."* came and went, the machine turned off. The test ended, and I felt as if I had just had a full night's sleep. It would be another two weeks before I knew the results.

I left the testing center with strange, lingering feelings. I had just relived the experience, but it felt more real and vibrant than ever. I had spent the morning completely immersed in the vision in my mind, and for the first time in a while, I felt deep relaxation. My body felt rested, and I was at peace.

Two weeks later, my name was called at the doctor's office. Connie and I followed the assistant into a small room with a large screen for x-rays. The neurologist, a quiet-spoken Asian woman, entered and asked several questions about the events that had led to our meeting.

I briefly explained that I had experienced a widow maker, received 1,200+ chest compressions, and had been in Vfib for approximately 20 minutes. She opened her computer and projected my EEG results onto the screen. Overall, they appeared relatively normal. She noted very minor signs of impairment, too small to quantify.

Then she opened the MRI images I had gone through. A full-color image of my brain appeared on the screen. Her first question was whether I had hit my head during the cardiac arrest. I hadn't experienced any direct physical trauma—just the absence of a heartbeat, with CPR being my only source of oxygen to the brain.

She pointed out two noticeable white areas toward the back of my brain. These, she explained, were old injuries—past concussions from years of ice hockey and fighting.

Then she gave me particularly good news. My brain showed no signs of anoxic brain injury. She was clearly surprised and told me that it was very unusual for someone to endure such a traumatic event without damage. I told her my mother had suffered from Alzheimer's and asked if there were any indicators of that in my brain. She explained that I showed remarkably few signs beyond what would be considered normal, and that I was fine.

I listened intently as she explained the different color regions on the images. I was amazed at how much she could determine from the scans. As I studied the screen, I noticed a very bright circle near the center of one image and asked her what it represented. She explained that during the test I had been experiencing a measurable emotional response in my brain. She said it was intense and sustained for a significant period of time. The area highlighted was associated with memory.

At that point, I asked if I could share what I had been experiencing during the scan. She smiled and said she was very interested. I described the memory in detail, from the beginning of the event all the way to the light. She was visibly surprised when I told her I had been reliving the entire experience during the imaging. She explained that this emotional recall was the source of the bright circle we were seeing.

Had we just captured an image of heaven? Was this a glimpse of God through science? What possible explanation could there be for such an intense brightness in the very area she said was so powerfully active? I was overwhelmed. They had captured, in real time, what I was seeing in my mind. It was real. I wasn't imagining it.

When I told her about the white envelope and the red fire trucks with their numbers on the side, she said there was no feasible way I could have known those details.

I was stunned and deeply moved all at once. I had just seen physical evidence of the recollection of my death on an actual MRI. It cemented the miracle for me. This doesn't happen. I felt the Holy Spirit fill my heart with a profound sense of purpose—though I didn't yet know what that purpose would be. What a majestic feeling it was to experience His presence through the lens of science. Faith and science are not mutually exclusive. I could feel His peace and sense His approval. God had spoken to me.

CHAPTER 12:
THEY CALL ME LAZARUS

All in all, I was progressing rather well for a guy who had died a couple of months earlier. Several more scans were done. Within two months following my cardiac arrest, I was starting to navigate the damage. The medications I was on made me tired all the time. Even though I was improving, I continued to carry the mental anguish of what felt like a ticking time bomb in my chest. I couldn't shake the fear of it happening again. When I felt off, I would check my blood pressure and find it consistently in the mid to high 80s. My heart rate was constantly in the low 40s.

Part of my physical makeup was that my vital signs were already low before the cardiac arrest. The medication I was taking was designed for someone with high blood pressure, as is often the case with heart attack victims. I was not the normal case. The doctors were initially perplexed because a man my age would typically show signs of plaque buildup or atherosclerosis from poor diet or lack of exercise. I had neither. I was told the healthy part of my heart looked like that of a 25-year-old. Eventually, I would be taken off the medication.

My life of extreme exercise and eating right worked in my favor during recovery, and it showed. The stents ensured I should be fine moving forward. All the scans and tests confirmed that I was healthy—except for the damaged portion of my heart caused by the STEMI. That damage was permanent, and nothing could be done about it. I made up my mind to improve what I could and move past the event. I was determined to get back to normal.

Normal. There's a word with many facets. What was my new normal? My mind questioned every ache and pain in my chest. I was showing signs of trauma-related stress from the entire experience. Inside, I was still only months removed from waking up in the ICU, and I was having some unbelievably hard conversations with myself. It was a constant mental tug-of-war—trying to show outward joy as someone who belonged to the 1% blessed with such a miracle, while inwardly, I sometimes longed to return to the light.

Sleep had always come easily to me. I would put in my earplugs, kiss Connie, tell her I loved her, and within seconds I'd be asleep, holding her hand. Now, months later, settling in was a struggle. My chest and back still carried considerable pain from the compressions, and the Zoll vest I was wearing constantly reminded me that it could go off at any moment—even in my sleep—and slam me in the chest.

The stress built slowly, like the story of the boiling frog. When the frog is placed in cool water, he doesn't notice a thing. As the heat rises gradually, the water becomes warm and comfortable. By the time it boils, he's too exhausted to jump out. That's when it's too late. Slowly, I was sinking into a mental place I never saw coming. I was struggling deeply with the fear of another cardiac arrest.

By all accounts from the professionals, I was miraculously going to be okay. But I had doubts. Why was I struggling so much if I was such a miracle? Shouldn't I be dancing on the rooftops? Would God save me from death just to saddle me with health problems? In all honesty, I was starting to subconsciously prefer the peace and quiet of the light I had seen. Increasingly, I would close my eyes and relive the entire video over and over.

All I had to do was shut my eyes, and there it was again. The entire scene would loop in my mind's eye, often bringing me to tears. Was I losing my mind? To prefer that memory was, in a way, to prefer death. I was still struggling with basic recall—names of objects that I could see clearly in my mind, yet couldn't speak; faces I recognized, but couldn't call by name. I made a living creating relationships, and I couldn't remember names!

If there was ever a time my human condition dictated my life, it was beginning to take hold. My mind wandered into dark places of shame—shame for wanting to return to that light and the peace it brought. Was all of this part of His plan? If it was, why so much stress and pain? I had been humbled by this miracle but didn't understand why. How could I rejoice when it felt like everything around me was unraveling? Did I truly experience a miracle, or was this some cruel joke?

I knew I needed to shake this despair off—but how? All my life, when challenges arose, I reminded myself to "Embrace the Suck," a concept many soldiers understand well. Gut it out, push through the pain; the reward is on the other side. I would tell myself, "It's not that bad. I've seen worse and persevered." But this time was different. I felt like I was slipping, starting to lose myself. I needed a handhold—something tangible, something that would allow me to see progress and move in the right direction again. Something to quiet the bad self-talk consuming me.

I've been blessed with the ability to set a goal and crush it. Usually, I start by visualizing myself completing the goal—seeing it in my mind first. Visualization has always been powerful for me. But this time, it was nearly impossible. The constant loop in my head acted like white noise, replaying endlessly—like a commercial on TV that never stopped. I would shut my eyes to sleep, only to wake up with it running again. It was maddening.

I wasn't sure if my memory issues were part of the problem, but concentrating was a challenge. I needed something simple, something achievable, to give me a sense of progress. I realized I had to start pulling myself together. At the time, it felt like I was starting my life over. Past successes seemed distant, and the thought of beginning again was daunting.

I had been going to cardio-rehab twice a week. The staff was welcoming and supportive, and their encouragement made me feel special. I pushed myself hard—I always took the stairs instead of the elevator and would talk about hockey, about how it always made me feel young. Then it hit me: *That's it!* I was going back to the rink. I was going to prove to the youngsters that Moses could part the waters again.

I still had a month left to wear the Zoll vest. During an appointment with my cardiologist, I asked him if I could go back and play hockey. He said there was no reason not to. I just needed to listen to my body. If I felt tired, I was to stop and rest. He trusted me not to overdo it.

I began focusing on the possibilities rather than the daunting symptoms I had been feeling. My brain switched gears and started talking me into what had once seemed impossible. I was learning a valuable lesson about my relationship with God. He is in complete charge, and when the time is right, He tells me. It is up to me to listen.

May 31st was the date I would be free from the Zoll vest. I was looking forward to that day. It felt like freedom—from the constant reminder that my heart could stop at any moment, and from the threat of a severe kick in the chest. My thoughts turned to my hockey stick. I took it out, felt the familiar length of it, tore off the tape, and retaped it just as I had done for the last fifty years. The simple act of holding that stick and wrapping tape around it completely rebooted my brain. I stopped thinking about my injured heart and started counting the days until I could skate again.

I returned my Zoll vest to my cardiologist's office on the way to the rink on May 31st, 2022. It had been three and a half months since I was lying in the street receiving CPR. I arrived early. No one was there yet. I took my time getting dressed in the locker room. My emotions were mixed. On one hand, I was scared to death—my heart was pounding in my chest. On the other, I was soaking in every ounce of joy, reflecting on how far I had come in just three months.

The last time I had been in this very place, I was about to die and didn't know it. My life would be forever altered. I brushed those thoughts aside and focused on putting on my equipment. Pulling my jersey over my pads made me breathe hard, reminding me how weak I had become. I reminded myself that I had been beaten up, slowed to a crawl, and that my heart was severely damaged—yet I had already come so far. What should I expect from this moment? Doubt began creeping in about whether I was returning too soon.

I've done difficult things in my life, but coming back from the dead to play hockey transcended them all. My faith in God, and my belief in my ability to accomplish hard things, was about to be tested once again. God had put me here to show His mercy and the true meaning of what a miracle really looks like.

The locker room door opened and someone walked in carrying a large hockey bag and a few sticks. It was the familiar face of one of my hockey buddies. He looked up, stopped in his tracks, and said, "What happened to you? I heard you died!"

I told him I had died in my car from a widow maker heart attack on the way home, right after we played several months earlier. He was visibly excited to see me. Just then, more people began to arrive.

Several of the guys piled in, and the reunion made my heart soar. "Moses, you're back!" I spent the rest of the time before hitting the ice explaining my journey. Some of the younger guys, in their thirties, were intensely interested in what a widow maker felt like. I explained that my symptoms had started while I was playing hockey with them—the heavy feeling, the disorientation. Not all symptoms are obvious, though.

I told them, as I had learned over time, that sometimes it just feels like a serious case of heartburn. Other symptoms can include a heaviness in the chest, like I was feeling that day. You can also experience pain in your left jaw, like a dull toothache. The process of the main artery clogging can take years, months, or days. I mentioned that I had felt major heart attack symptoms immediately after my second Covid-19 vaccination. I was certain I had a heart attack for about 18 hours after receiving the shot.

The following day, I felt better, with no symptoms. It's hard to know when your artery is clogging. High blood pressure can be a precursor to heart disease. In my case, I have exceptionally low blood pressure and heart rate. There were few signs of heart disease even after my cardiac arrest. All the tests left the cardiologists a bit perplexed. At first, it was rarely spoken aloud that the Covid-19 shot might be the culprit. Over time, it became the working conclusion: the anomalous clot that clogged my major artery was highly likely caused by the vaccine. Many of my hockey buddies hadn't taken the vaccine. A few had, and they were visibly worried.

Some of my earliest memories come from being on the ice—the sound of my skates crunching, the musty smell of ice that had been resurfaced, the hum of the machine smoothing the rink. I was back, and my heart and mind felt aligned again. I had made it back to where I once was. Maybe not as whole as I used to be, but I had returned.

The locker room chirping started up immediately. "Maybe we shouldn't call you Moses." "How about Jesus? Or Lazarus?" Lazarus it was. I am now Lazarus—raised from the dead to play hockey again. What an honor to be part of such a salty group of misfits. I was back where I belonged. Time to play. Drop the puck!

Stepping onto the ice felt like I had been gone for years. My skates felt unfamiliar. My hips were stiff, my lower back ached, and my shoulders were weak. I was out of breath. I became aware that I was not the solid, athletic self I once was. Still, I continued to pass the puck and skate. It felt incredible to hear the crunch of my skate blades on the ice again. For the first time in months, the stress of living with a ticking time bomb in my chest had subsided.

There weren't as many guys as usual, which meant more ice time and less bench rest. The lack of rest caught up with me quickly. I was tired. After two months of cardio rehab, I thought I was in decent shape. Apparently, I was out of hockey shape. I told myself to slow down, focus on breathing, and enjoy the moment. My cardio watch suddenly read 150 beats per minute— I don't think I had ever seen it that high.

Sitting on the bench, looking at my high heart rate, brought back the familiar fear and paranoia. I reminded myself to slow down and enjoy the achievement. I thought of advice from a climbing guide on the Grand Teton in 1978, when I had been panicking about how I'd get down: *"Stop and take a picture of the moment you achieve what you worked so hard for; you may never achieve it again."* To this day, I treasure the memory of stepping back on that ice. It was a milestone. I thanked God: *"Dear God, I rejoice in Your mercy and grace. Thank You for making me a miracle to demonstrate Your majestic power."*

I finished my time on the ice just talking to my friends. We stood around, holding our sticks, sharing stories. This is what I've always loved about the game. You can play hard, get chirped relentlessly, and still be friends in the end. Getting undressed in the locker room continued with stories and banter. I took my time soaking it all in. Inside, I felt alive again—more so than I had in months.

I continued to play more often over the next few months. The nickname Lazarus stuck, and we were always glad to see each other every time we met. My back, however, began to cause problems. I started experiencing serious cramping in the lower middle area. My inner right hip began to feel as though I had some kind of muscle tear. This was unusual for me, as I had always had solid legs. Now, after each game, I was suffering for a day or two afterward.

The hip pain grew more severe. Eventually, both hips were experiencing sharp, nerve-like pain. I began missing hockey more frequently. Before long, I was barely going at all because I paid dearly afterward with intense hip pain. Whatever was happening was not improving.

I started having trouble getting in and out of my car. At first, sitting for long periods became difficult. As time went on, I couldn't lift my knees high enough to get out of the car. I had to reach behind my legs and physically lift them out from under the steering wheel. Eventually, I couldn't stand up without assistance after getting out of the car. The pain had become unbearable.

CHAPTER 13:
TIME FOR A CANE

How do I adequately describe pain? This pain was so searing it would take my breath away—so devastating that it brought me to the edge of completely giving up. I had enjoyed good health and a strong body my entire life. My body had always been the vehicle for success. I must admit, I took it completely for granted.

I believed I was invincible. If I pushed through pain with perseverance, I could not be defeated. Pain was just weakness leaving my body. "Embrace the suck—the reward will be tenfold." From ice hockey and its bumps and bruises to simple injuries, the answer was always the same: tape it up and get back out there.

Two knee surgeries didn't stop me. I would skate harder, longer, build the muscle back, and keep going. There was always a tryout, always something ahead. My solution was always, *"There's always tomorrow. Get busy."*

I earned my first-degree black belt while irrigating cotton twelve hours a night in the desert heat. I would take my boots off, set my hat on the hood of my truck, and practice every form all night long. When it was time to move the irrigation to the next border, I'd put my boots and hat back on and return to hard physical labor. Once finished, I'd kick them off again and start practicing all over.

I repeated this cycle day and night. I was at the top of my class. I had everything memorized almost immediately, while the rest of the class took months. While others were still learning, I was refining and mastering technique. This level of demanding work felt natural to me. I had mastered the art of embracing the suck. I was strong, capable, and a born leader because I could master physical challenges quickly.

That ability led to an exceptionally long and successful career teaching martial arts to civilians. My capacity to master physical skills quickly put me far ahead of the police and military personnel I trained. Simply put, I put exponentially more effort into learning techniques that led to true mastery. I was often rejected by law enforcement officers I trained. They struggled with stepping out of their role as enforcers and into the role of students under a civilian—especially one who was a better fighter and shooter than they were.

I addressed that reality directly from the beginning, bypassing the egos involved—mine included.

Injury was part of the job. Over the years, I sustained fractures to both hands, both feet, my collarbone, nose, and sternum. I suffered two concussions, three knee surgeries, three shoulder operations, a severed Achilles tendon, and a complete shoulder replacement. I tore three major muscle groups. I was struck by ricochet bullets three times and slashed across the wrist with a live blade. I fell thirty feet during a rock climb and was forced to downclimb facing outward on my heels with both feet broken. The list goes on.

I came to understand exactly where my pain threshold lived.

Nothing can describe the level of excruciating nerve pain I was experiencing in my back and both hips. The compressions I received had somehow caused a rib bone to dislocate and saw against a nerve. This, in turn, caused the muscles in both legs to atrophy. I went from 220 pounds to 175, losing forty-five pounds—forty-five pounds of muscle. I was now walking on two severely arthritic hips and damaged nerves. I could no longer lift my knees. Driving became impossible.

My main activity as a real estate agent is conducting open houses. I have done well over 2,500 in my career. I am very effective at building relationships, and this has always been the quickest way for me to meet real people. Unfortunately, it also required physical work—placing signs and standing for hours at a time. Connie was conscripted into the sign-placing business, dropping me off at the house while she handled the setup. I would try to find homes that were furnished with at least one chair to sit on, or I would bring a folding chair of my own.

My physical health quickly degraded to the point where I needed a cane, then a walker. I was simply losing my ability to walk. I don't believe in taking pain pills. I did take medicinal cannabis, prescribed and carefully dosed by my doctor, but it only allowed me to partially sleep through the night. We lived in a two-story home with the master bedroom upstairs. The stairs became the greatest challenge. I was now a serious fall risk, and those stairs were about to become my biggest obstacle.

Connie would help me climb them one step at a time as I essentially did push-ups using the railing and my cane. By the time I reached the top, I was completely exhausted.

That simple trip upstairs often left me in tears, writhing in pain. I was trying to walk on bare bone while pinching both sciatic nerves. My hips were dislocating due to the lack of muscle and would become caught out of joint. I would be forced to lie flat on my back on the floor while Connie attempted to pull each leg bone out of the hip socket and guide it back into place. A loud pop would follow—then searing pain, and finally brief relief.

I was spiraling downward. *"Dear God, why am I here if You wanted me to live?"* What possible message was I being sent? I was nearing the end of my strength and willpower. I was living in the worst human condition I could imagine. Where was the miracle in this?

Connie felt every scream and endured every tear. She never left my side. I was completely unbearable at times. I would often explode in frustration. Often, Connie was right in the path of my destruction. She was the constant, eternal optimist. She refused to let me disparage myself or speak in defeat.

I vividly remember one moment when I angrily shouted at her to just listen to me. I was fully immersed in defeat. She would have none of it. I was the lone attendee at my own pitiful party. Looking back now, I realize her will for me to survive was unshakable. She had angels on her side, fighting for me. She was invincible.

Life was beginning to slow around me. I was slipping into a dark pit of hopelessness. My prayers felt unanswered. Had God abandoned me to figure this out on my own? Was this the lesson of my rebirth? My world was growing darker, day slowly turning into night. Every time I faced those stairs, I was acutely aware of how weak I had become.

I had two walkers—one upstairs and one downstairs. My cane was the only support I had to get between them. My hands and elbows ached so badly I could barely hold anything. I wanted desperately to be normal again, but normal was a distant memory. My life as a strong, independent fighter had been shelved and replaced with someone I barely recognized—a man who no longer wanted to face the light he had once been shown.

I couldn't see the miracle right in front of me. Everything dissolved into simple day-to-day survival. We were running out of money, and I was mustering everything I had just to get dressed and sit through an open house. To make matters worse, it was the summer of 2022, and the real estate market was grinding to a halt under runaway inflation and soaring interest rates.

I would sit at an open house, hoping someone friendly would walk through the door. I greeted them cane in hand. I'm certain my demeanor was neither friendly nor energetic. I needed to sell a house—quickly. I had fallen into the trap of selling instead of relationship building, the very trap I taught new agents to avoid. People can smell desperation when you're selling something. Looking back, I suspect I reeked of it. Life was becoming exceedingly difficult, fast.

By the end of a typical open house, I was in excruciating pain and desperate to get home. Connie would pick me up after retrieving the signs and the heavy sandbags that held them in place. I would sit in silence on the drive home. I had just spent six lonely hours in pain. My efforts felt worthless, yet this was all I had to try and generate business.

Connie was trying so hard to lift me up. She needed me to be better—and soon. Our life depended on me doing what I had always done best: creating relationships and serving my customers. But I was no longer in the shape to do either, mentally or physically.

I sat through open houses on Saturdays and Sundays. The rest of the week was spent watching time and money slip away. Pills in the morning, pills at lunch, pills at dinner. Climb the stairs and have Connie pull my legs back into place. More pills, then into bed with pain. She would watch television to block out her own worry and fear.

I was in real trouble and didn't know how to say it out loud. The heavenly light I had experienced was present in nearly every thought. I began carrying a deep shame for wanting to be back there again—even if it meant being without Connie.

The two commissions I was able to earn the week after my cardiac arrest were finally running out. We had exhausted our savings. I reached out to friends and coworkers for solutions. The realtor organization I belonged to provided an emergency fund. They teach and support active Realtors. They gave us enough money to pay a month's bills. Several church organizations stepped up with food and some cash. A friend started a GoFundMe that brought in much-needed money for bills and groceries. I sold my car; I wasn't driving anyway. We were broke financially. I was broken mentally.

It was decided that Connie would step up and work at a grocery delivery service. I was there to help in any way I could, but in general, I was more in the way. She would get an order for groceries, and I would follow her into the store on the electric scooters at the front. The service had a general location in the store to find the specific grocery order. Connie would send me off on my scooter and cane to locate as much as I could and meet her to go through the line and pay.

Easier said than done. We were on the clock, and it was ticking. The person who ordered would add something just as we were about to pay, or they would want some obscure baby food item, flavor, or size. We would be rushing around like two crazy old people. The orders were on an app on her phone. Let me tell you, we both hate those apps. They are so confusing, yet we had to learn on the go under the gun. If divorce was ever imminent, it was in aisle 10 looking for that silly baby food. Today, that period in our marriage is a source of somewhat painful but hearty laughter.

In the midst of all this struggle, we would get a call from our daughter needing us to pick up a grandson and drop the other at a location. We tried to keep our difficulty private, so it should have been expected that it didn't make sense to her the stress we had. Our world was spinning out of control—and here we were delivering groceries. This was the only method a couple of 60+ year-olds had to put cash together to simply survive.

It was time to start selling our things. The months were cruising faster than we could keep up financially. I wasn't getting better, and Connie was doing all she could do. We were drowning in basic bills—rent, food, gas, utilities, and phones. We just didn't have enough.

I have always been attached to the things I acquired and gave to Connie. We were about to launch garage sales and liquidate our personal belongings. It started with my musical instruments and equipment. Everything was to go eventually except a guitar I bought when I was just nine years old. Music had consumed me up to this point. It was a very large part of my identity. I was a musician without music now. The only real tangible memory of my music was a few videos on stage and music I had written. I held tightly to the memory of my mother and the song, *"Tomorrow Has Just Begun."*

I didn't know at the time just how amazing that title was. My mother, in her fog of Alzheimer's, had bestowed upon me the wisest words I had ever heard. God had saved me for a purpose so much bigger than myself. I was undergoing a massive transformation of spirit and faith. The trials we went through were indeed the necessary foundation of something much bigger. The hidden lessons of pain and devastation were the framework of my future. As I look back, tomorrow truly had begun.

We sold pictures and furniture. We sold household items from the kitchen. We sold our wedding china. All the things Connie had gathered and placed around us so beautifully were gone. The walls were bare. The table was gone. We had one couch left. We sold TVs. Next was jewelry. Connie had beautiful jewelry I had bought her over the years—gone. Next were the wedding rings—gone. Garden furniture—gone. Everything—gone.

We still had each other. We never gave up on us. I was in the worst place mentally by this point. I felt like I had caused all of this. It was my fault. I couldn't function anymore to keep us afloat. I had lost all worth as a man, and I didn't know how to find myself again. Connie continued delivering groceries without me, as I could hardly get in and out of a car and it was easier for her to do it alone. I sat at home feeling sorry for myself while she worked her tail off. I have never known a stronger woman.

Our human condition had taken everything away from us. We had nothing left but a bed, a television, and a few miscellaneous items. Our closets were bare. The refrigerator was bare. We were getting help from a local church with some staple food and small items. The GoFundMe dribbled in enough money to buy gas and keep the lights on. Christmas was canceled except for the boys. We put up a tree we hadn't sold and tried to make the best of it.

CHAPTER 14:
ONE MORE MIRACLE

Throughout the financial trials, my hips continued to completely disintegrate. I was heading for a wheelchair. I had already been given a disabled parking placard so I could get to the store more easily, but I was no longer driving. Something had to give. I decided to see an orthopedic surgeon. He confirmed the inevitable. I had bone-on-bone arthritis in both hips. It wasn't going to get any better.

Insurance being insurance, I had to undergo a series of three steroid injections in each hip before they would authorize replacements. All this did was delay my relief. I scheduled the first set of injections. I am not the biggest fan of needles to begin with. While waiting for the procedure, I shared my story of the Widow Maker with the nurse. She cried when I repeated my mother's words, "Not yet, not yet." I took a moment to tell her about the song I had published for my mother. She wrote the name of the song, *"Tomorrow Has Just Begun,"* on a Post-it note and left the room.

When it was time for the procedure, the doctor ushered me back. I entered a room filled with monitors and X-ray machines positioned over a table where I would lie. You should see the size of the harpoon they use. The needle they were about to stick in my backside sat on a tray. I could feel my heart rate pick up. They sensed I was nervous. The nurse asked if they could play some music during the procedure. I said, "Sure."

In that very moment, I heard the harmonic ping of the opening E note of my song. They were playing my song. God had just stepped in to soothe my soul. I will never forget that day. I instantly felt a sense of self-worth return. How could they know how much I had lost? That song meant so much to me. It could never be taken from me.

The song was mine, and it would forever remind me of my mother. Here she was again, telling me to calm down. Everything was going to be all right. The entire song played. Everyone in the room was moved—some to tears—as I explained that the essence of my mother's last smile was built into that song. The procedure was over quickly. I felt some relief from the lidocaine mixed into the injection. That day felt like the beginning of the end of the nightmare I had been living.

During the ride home, I told Connie about them playing the song. I couldn't hold back my tears. I felt so broken and tired. After all we had been through, it felt like it was never going to end. Yet the title of the song kept playing in my mind: *Tomorrow Has Just Begun.* I prayed it was true.

My hips continued to be unbearable. Along with the injections, I was given physical rehabilitation to endure. No amount of exercise was going to relieve the excruciating pain I was experiencing, although the therapists were amazing. They heard my story and put great care into my rehabilitation. The hour twice a week was a double-edged sword. I enjoyed getting out of the house. On the other hand, I dreaded the pain of stretching and pushing through nerves that were constantly on fire.

No number of injections or exercises was going to address what was going on in my head, though. What had happened to me? Where did I go? I couldn't sit or stand long enough to play music. I didn't have anything left to play it with anyway. Sitting at open houses was becoming a hazard. I was completely a fall risk. One hard bump to the head could cause severe bleeding in my brain due to the blood thinners I was taking. Because of the blood pressure medication, my heart rate was dropping to 38, and my blood pressure would at times fall to dangerously low levels. I was extremely unstable from the searing pain in both hips. I didn't know it at the time, but I was about to be given a new identity and purpose.

Sometimes, just standing up, I would black out for a moment until my heart caught up. When it did, my hips were so unstable I felt like I was going to tip over. I was becoming a paranoid wreck. All I wanted to do was lie on the bed and sleep. I would fall asleep at open houses. I would fall asleep in the morning. I took naps three to four times a day. I could not muster an ounce of motivation. I wasn't sure whether my problem was physical or mental. The doctors said I was progressing and that my heart was stable. My mind was telling me something very different.

I prayed constantly for clarity of purpose. I had not lost sight of the fact that I had been blessed with a miracle. I just wasn't listening to the purpose God was putting before me each day. That purpose was veiled in hardship for my wife. My purpose was hidden in the excruciating nerve pain that was stealing my ability to walk. My purpose was in our empty bank account. It was there when I felt lost. God was speaking to me as I felt alone and defeated, doing a job I once loved. My cane and my walkers defined my purpose. I was sitting in the dark, right next to the light switch. Where had I gone? Would I ever return to what used to be normal? I pulled on my faith as hard as I could. I was trying to hear His voice, but my own inner voice was drowning out the answer.

Six weeks later, another session of injections followed, along with more physical therapy. I was getting worse, not better. The cane became my constant companion. My palms and hands ached constantly from using the walker. Standing for any length of time was unbearable. The slightest bump could knock me over. I couldn't sit on a bench watching my grandsons play hockey. My hands hurt so badly that I couldn't tie their skates. I didn't want to show them my pain, but it would surface anyway.

Connie and I would take care of the boys as needed; it was my favorite time. Being around their zany enthusiasm seemed to dull my pain a bit. Wherever they needed to go, Connie and I would take them together. I would sit and squirm through hockey practices. Hockey games had become our primary source of entertainment. The trips to and from school were filled with excited conversation. They seemed oblivious to the cane Papa now needed to use. It's funny how adaptable children are. God was showing me my purpose through them as well.

What exactly was that purpose? Was I given a second chance to be a better husband, father, and grandfather? Was I meant to become someone so pitiful that I would be humbled? Possibly I was to start everything over and become someone completely different. Or maybe I was to remain the same person God made me to be. Just who that person was supposed to be—that was the question.

Just after my second round of injections, a very powerful moment occurred. After meeting the two police officers who performed CPR on me, I had put great effort into locating the people involved in my miracle. One man in particular was responsible for pulling me out of my car while Angel was waving her arms at anyone who would stop. They were all angels—every single one of them.

It was now October 2022, eight months after my cardiac arrest, when my phone rang. I saw the caller ID and realized it was the man I had tried to find through social media back in February. I had messaged him then, asking him to please call me, but I never heard back—until now.

I answered the phone and said, "Thanks, man!" After a short pause, I heard a quiet and slightly confused hello. I asked him if he had pulled a man out of his car on Valentine's Day. He said yes. I told him that man was me. He replied, "They said you died."

"Nope," I said. "Here I am."

We spoke briefly and agreed to meet the following Saturday at my favorite coffee house, 4 Silos, in Gilbert.

I called the firehouse that had responded and asked if they could show up with the engine on Saturday. I was on a mission to thank every one of my lifesavers. He was all in. Watching the faces of the people who saw me alive and well is a memory I will never forget. The look on each face told their story. At some point, each of them had likely recalled to a friend or coworker the "Widow Maker dude" who died on their shift. And now here I was—in the flesh—smiling and hugging them. Priceless.

Saturday morning dawned clear, the start of what would become an amazing day. I arrived on time and was ordering an iced tea when I looked over and saw a tall, thin man in his fifties walk through the door. He stopped and just stared at me for a moment. Then came joyful hugs and tears with a man who had listened to God and stopped that day. I was holding my cane and squeezing him tightly. I am in tears as I write this. To see, in person, the figure who had been playing on a loop in my mind was incredible.

As we greeted each other and prepared to sit down, the fire engine rolled up and hit the siren. Everybody in the coffee shop turned to see the commotion. The entire team of firefighters walked in and gave us both hugs and handshakes. My favorite fireman made a presentation to my new friend and thanked him for being a prize citizen of Gilbert. Without his help, I would have died in the street that day. My purpose was beginning to peek through the clouds of my depression and pain.

The two of us sat and began to talk. He was in utter disbelief. Before he described his experience, I told him about the looping video in my mind. I explained that every time I met another person involved in my rescue, I described to them the movie playing in my head. He listened intently as I described the light pole and how I was looking down from above.

I relayed the entire scene and asked what caused him to be there that day. He explained that he worked for a builder and was very familiar with Higley Road. For some reason, that day he was on the wrong end of the road. He felt compelled to head south instead of north, though he couldn't explain why. He saw Angel waving for help and initially thought she was having car trouble. He pulled over, and she looked frantic.

He described me as purple, with foam coming out of my mouth. I was tangled in the seatbelt. He managed to pull me from the car, and Angel began CPR. During our conversation, I asked what his wife had thought about it all. He said she believed it was a miracle that he stopped. At the time, he couldn't see the miracle in it—after all, I had died, or so they had been told.

For eight months, he believed in his heart that I was indeed dead. Until his wife checked his direct messages. She had been right all along—it was a miracle that he stopped. I asked what his wife thought about our meeting now. He agreed that she had faith in God, and she was right again. God had delivered him to me.

We continued to talk for quite some time, sharing stories about our lives. We both had incredible wives, and we were both blessed with amazing grandchildren. I will forever remember this man as the person who was there to continue my purpose.

Just before we parted, I asked him if he wanted another miracle. He nodded. I described to him the exact details of where he was parked and what he was wearing that day. His eyes filled with tears as I described his shirt and the logo on it. He said quietly, "That's my work shirt." God is so good. Another person saw His light that day. God was telling me something.

One more miracle.

He had come to believe in the power of God that day, and I trust that impression will stay with him. Each time I met someone directly involved in my human condition that day, a miracle of faith followed. It was hard to deny—I was not supposed to be there. Yet there I was, telling them where they were standing and what they were doing. How often does God show Himself with such definitive detail? When was the last time God spoke to you, but you didn't hear Him?

CHAPTER 15:
YOU PROMISED ME GOD

My third set of injections was scheduled for February 2023. I was nearing the one-year anniversary of my cardiac arrest—my first re-birthday. Many times, when a person has experienced clinical death, they refer to the day they regain their life as a re-birthday.

I had endured intense highs and devastating lows. We were now on the verge of losing everything. Our money had completely run out. Connie was working seven days a week delivering food. It was destroying her—and our only car. She came home exhausted every night. I was useless in the fight. Every morning and every night, she had to pull my legs back into socket to reset the joint. I was melting right in front of her.

I was losing faith. My miracle had turned into my nightmare. The third set of injections once again proved useless. Physical therapy caused more pain than relief. I felt completely hopeless. Would I ever find my way through this? When would my hip replacements be approved? Would I ever walk again? The days became torture. I had lost myself and began having very dark thoughts.

I was slipping deeper into pain and depression, yet God was having a constant conversation with me—I just wasn't listening. I was consumed by my human condition. I had lost my purpose. I was in pain. The fear of another cardiac arrest filled my thoughts. My world was collapsing daily.

The question *why me* played on repeat like a broken record. And through it all, the light and my mother's words—*"Not yet, not yet"*—echoed in my mind.

On Valentine's Day 2023, one year after my widow maker, I made an appointment to meet a dear realtor friend for lunch. She worked at the real estate office on the south side of the street where I had died in my car a year earlier. I remembered clusters of people lined up on the sidewalk that day, watching emergency vehicles as they tried to revive me. The office parking lot was on the same side of the street.

As I sat in the foyer waiting for my friend, I closed my eyes and relived the entire experience. The video that played in my head was still in full color—just as vivid as it had been from the beginning.

The office manager was very chatty—pleasant and outgoing. Greeting people suited her perfectly. I could tell she had worked there a long time. I asked if she had been working the previous Valentine's Day. She said she had been there for many years and never missed a day. I asked if she remembered the emergency scene out front around 1:30 that day a year ago.

She said she did. Most of the office staff had gone outside to watch. I asked if she knew what had happened. She said it was terrible—a man had died in his car at the stoplight. The police were doing CPR for what felt like forever before the fire department arrived. Traffic was backed up, and police cars blocked the road so emergency crews could work.

I asked her if she knew what ultimately happened to the man. She said the CPR went on endlessly. They could see the man's feet moving beneath the car. The police told her it didn't look like he made it. The fire department shocked him several times, then finally loaded him into the ambulance.

I looked at her and said, "He lived."

Her expression changed instantly. She asked me if I had been there. I said, "I am that man." Her face went pale. She said it must have been a different day—*that* man had died at the scene. The police and fire department said so.

"Nope," I replied. "They brought me back, and here I am. God is real. Miracles happen every day, and heaven is indescribable. Don't go away— I'll be right back."

She disappeared and returned moments later with a dozen coworkers. "It's him!" she exclaimed.

They stood there stunned. I said, "Yep, it's me. I was up on that light pole right there, watching the whole thing." I proceeded to describe where everyone had been standing. I even mentioned a green car parked in front of the office.

The office manager shrieked, "That was *my* car! How could you possibly know that?" For the next fifteen minutes, I shared my story with the entire office. Every one of them was completely shaken.

Being given the opportunity to share my story has been one of the few saving graces during this season. I never shy away from describing God's magnificent glory. The video still lives in my mind as if it happened yesterday. When I feel lost or overwhelmed, it becomes a source of hope— a reminder of the miracle I was given and that I still have a purpose to fulfill.

The light never faded. I was constantly aware of it. The sound of my mother's voice. The entire scene replayed endlessly in my mind. I was ashamed of myself because I wanted to die. I wanted to go back to the light. The longing consumed me. Would God forgive me for feeling this way? All I could think about was the peace—the complete and total comfort I had experienced. That place had no boundaries. I had been surrounded by heavenly light and perfect peace.

Now my life felt like a nightmare.

March of 2023 dragged on relentlessly. Wake up in pain. Therapy brought more pain. Connie drove seven days a week just to keep the lights on. Friends helped us find resources for food and utilities. Car payments were always late. I juggled what little I could. Seven-dollar meals required creativity. A local Christian charity provided food bank staples—thin and sparse, but received with deep humility.

I couldn't even consider holding an open house anymore. In my mind and heart, I was useless. It crushed me to watch Connie fight every day just to bring home barely enough to survive. She carried the entire load. I felt like nothing more than a burden.

I woke up Saturday, April 1st, like any other morning—depressed and in pain. Connie was already downstairs preparing for another long day. She would work half the day, come home briefly, then go back out until after dark.

Before she left, she made me a sandwich, grabbed some chips, and told me to stay upstairs. I was a hazard on the stairs by myself.

Normally, if I had to go upstairs, Connie would push from behind as I climbed—lifting my legs with one hand, gripping the railing with the other, cane in hand. I would have to stop and rest often. Going down was difficult. Going up was the Hillary Step of Mount Everest.

That day, she brought me my sandwich, chips, a piece of fruit, and a couple of cookies. I was to stay in bed and rest while watching TV. Our standard poodle, Gibson, stayed with me—my constant companion.

Connie left, and I was alone again.

I ate my lunch and lay there watching television. Then I wanted something sweet. The cookies she had made were calling to me from the downstairs closet. That craving pushed me out of bed and toward the stairs. I left my walker behind and took only my cane.

Gibson slowly followed me as I navigated from one stair to the next, cane in hand. I arrived downstairs and switched to the walker placed at the bottom of the stairs. The kitchen was only a few steps from the pantry. I planned to have some cookies and watch the downstairs TV for a bit. Eventually, I fell asleep on the couch and sank into a heavy nap. When I woke, I was sluggish and stiff with pain. I remember the next half hour like it was yesterday.

I walked with my walker to the stairs, my cane hanging from the handlebars. At the steps, I switched back to the cane. Gibson was now in front of me. I moved painfully slow, pushing myself up the first flight of stairs. The next flight required a right-hand turn up a short stoop. About two steps into that second flight, my feet got tangled. I slipped and suddenly found myself crumpled, half upside down, with my hips twisted beneath me.

The pain from both hips at once made me dizzy. I was out of breath, and my right arm—the one with the shoulder implant—was trapped underneath me. I was completely stuck. I couldn't push myself up or lift enough to reach my cane, which I had dropped one step below me. I needed it desperately, but I couldn't reach it. My hips were screaming.

I tried with everything I had to turn myself over, but that meant rolling onto my already twisted hips. I was becoming exhausted. No matter how hard I tried, I couldn't get my weight off my hips from that angle. I attempted to slide down the stairs, but that only twisted me further.

Panic set in. My heart was racing. Pain consumed my shoulder and hips. Time seemed to disappear—I had been there far too long. I started to fear another cardiac event. I was gasping for breath, and I could hear my heart pounding in my head.

Finally, I managed to pull my arm out from underneath me and slide headfirst down a few stairs on my back. I ended up stuck upside down— head lower than my feet. Blood rushed to my head. What a predicament. I was exhausted and in throbbing pain. I must have spent twenty minutes just to get to this point.

I continued sliding until I reached the midway landing. I sat there, trying to gather myself. The pain was indescribable. It felt like an electric taser firing nonstop into both hips.

I grabbed my cane and tried to lift myself. My arms were completely spent. It was all I could do to get to my knees. I was crying and furious at the same time. I had just about had enough.

I prepared myself for the climb ahead. For another fifteen minutes, I wedged myself in and pulled up, step by step, using my cane. My legs were useless. Gibson waited at the top of the stairs, his front paws draped over the edge, head down—as if to say, *I'm here for you, but you have to get up here.*

By now I was crying and swearing out loud. I was alone. I was angry beyond words. Completely exhausted. Ready to give up altogether.

I finally reached the top of the stairs. It was ten feet to my bedroom door and five feet to the bed. I was sobbing and cursing—cursing at God. The very reason I was alive. The miracle I had been given came from Him, and here I was, screaming at Him. My purpose felt lost.

I crawled into bed and lay on my back, crying and swearing. I will never forget shouting at the top of my lungs:

"God, you promised me. Please save me!"

For several weeks I had been having very dark thoughts. They centered on the peace I had left behind and the desire to go back. I would shake myself out of it, ashamed of what that meant. I had become nothing in my own estimation. It was selfish of me, I know, but I was done trying to be brave. I was finished with the searing pain of Connie pulling my hips out of socket just to move the bone away from the nerves being crushed inside my hip sockets.

The moment had come. Today was the day. *I am so sorry, Connie. You don't deserve this.*

I cried out one last time to God. "God, you promised me! I repent, I repent, I repent. Please save me!"

At that very moment, the phone rang.

I looked at the caller ID. It was a close friend and former client. I wiped my face, took a breath, and answered in a low voice. "Hello?"

He asked how I was doing. "Unbelievable," I replied. He asked about my health. I told him I was doing wonderfully and getting better every day. I had just cussed out God, and now I was talking to someone I had sold a house to nine months earlier. He told me the reason for his call—he was getting married and needed me to sell his house immediately. He was under contract on another home and had to sell before he could close.

I asked when he wanted to go on the market. "Immediately," he said. Mind you, I hadn't sold a house in a year.

Within three days, his home was on the market. It was beautiful, though the market had allowed very little equity. I was concerned about it selling—until I hung up the phone.

What had just happened? The moment I cried out to God, the phone rang. That's what happened.

He had been with me the entire time. My Angel of Mercy lifted me off that stairwell. I wanted to end my life that day. I was done. No more. I cried out, and God said, "Not yet. Not yet."

If there was ever a moment of clarity of purpose, it was the second I hung up the phone. God had just presented Himself to me in the most profound way.

God is real. Miracles happen every day. Heaven is indescribable.

The light in my mind was brighter than ever. *Follow the light, Kevin. Follow the light.*

I had been shaped through such hardship that it took cursing God to finally see it clearly. I had fully acquiesced to His power and mercy. His grace was on full display.

God had seen me grow weary. He was with me on those stairs—right when I asked for His help, unorthodox as it may have been. There was more to come. I was done making the rules. I would follow His.

My self-talk shifted from depression to an ongoing conversation with the Holy Spirit within me. God is not done with me yet—just as He is not done with you.

Within days, the house was live. That same day, I received notice that my first hip replacement surgery was scheduled for the end of April. The left hip first, the right six weeks later.

Connie and I were ecstatic with relief. The hip saga was finally coming to an end.

I wasn't even sure the listing would sell. Then I caught myself—how about I put my faith back where it belongs?

My human condition had driven me to despair. Faith restored me. What had I learned? Every time crisis struck and I reached out, I was saved. I was beginning to understand that trials were not punishment, but preparation. God wanted me as His child. I simply had to accept it fully.

The house had one showing. One.

They bought it at full price. No concessions. No requests. My client recovered his down payment. I earned a full commission—paid the day before my surgery.

God took me from dead broke and ready to give up, to enough money to get caught up and survive both surgeries. You cannot make this up.

From the beginning, my journey has been a series of divine interventions— never early, never late. Always precisely when needed. I was wrapped in His garment of love and security.

The first hip was replaced. I walked out of the hospital the next morning. Anesthesia was the only challenge—I don't wake well from deep sleep. The procedure was done with robotic assistance. Thinking about the saws and hammers alone makes you cringe. But the pain was gone.

The only discomfort came from the thirty stainless steel staples holding me together.

I returned home wearing compression socks to prevent blood clots. Connie helped me with them every day. I was back in physical therapy the following week. The therapists—who had known me for so long—were overjoyed. I had become their "special patient."

Each time I shared my story with a new therapist, they would tear up, pause, and ask questions. I formed a bond with every one of them.

It was time for the staples to come out. I didn't exactly know what to expect. While I waited for the nurse practitioner to come in, I was looking over professional hockey scores and standings on my phone.

She entered the room and introduced herself. I was wearing a hockey T-shirt, and she asked if I was a fan. She was too. I told her my story—about hockey and my cardiac arrest. She teared up and said I had just helped her understand something. Her father had recently suffered a cardiac arrest and passed away. She said she was now certain he had been in nothing but peace and serenity.

She sat close and asked if I was ready. Out came the craziest-looking pliers. The first staple sent me through the roof.

She distracted me by asking questions about the NHL standings, then plucked another one out.

"How did the Coyotes do?" "They did goooooooood!"

"Are you a fan of Las Vegas?" "Noooooooooot really!"

This went on for twenty-eight more staples. I was laughing hysterically between screeches of skin-ripping pain. She was the best.

Surprisingly, the next six weeks flew by. I had to take another blood test to make sure my A1C levels were good. They were exactly the same as before. The test was to rule out pre-diabetes—major joint replacement surgery doesn't heal well if diabetes is present.

I was cleared and ready for the next one. I was already shopping for a new hockey stick.

My second hip replacement was done on June 8, 2023. Everything went even better than the first. This time I was given anti-nausea medication, which solved the issue I'd had previously. I felt confident and calm. All the fear and unknowns were gone. I was ready to move on.

I arrived, was prepped, and waited. This was supposed to be the end of the hardest period of my life. My heart was stable. My hips were about to be complete and pain-free. I could finally get on with my physical, mental, and spiritual life again.

It was over—or so I thought.

CHAPTER 16:
WHAT JUST HAPPENED?

The second hip surgery was completely routine. I was in for another twelve weeks of physical therapy. I was diligent, doing my exercises at home, before and after therapy days. There was plenty of suck to embrace, but I was all in. The end of the tunnel was in sight. The worst was behind me.

The stairs became exercise instead of impossibility.

I doubled my exercises. I wanted my strength back. I had a destiny with a hockey rink—and that new stick. I began gaining weight and muscle again. My thigh muscles had withered down to the size of my lower legs, and I had a long road before they were ready for ice skates.

I'd had three knee surgeries. I could rehab two new hips. I was motivated. The only pain I felt was good pain. Muscle soreness is a gift.

On July 7th—one month after my second hip replacement—I woke up early and rushed to the toilet. I was about to throw up. What was happening? I hadn't vomited in over a decade.

I had violent dry heaves. Nothing came up. I took a Maalox and went back to bed…. Nope. Not done.

I went back at least eight times. It felt like I was trying to throw up a baseball—nothing would come out.

I sat on the edge of the bed. Connie woke up and asked what was going on. I told her something was wrong. I felt off. I said we should go to the emergency room.

No questions. We both shifted into action.

I sensed the worry in her, but I tried to downplay it. "It's probably nothing. We'll be right back." We let the dog out and headed for the car.

I told her she should drive in case I had to vomit again. Other than the nausea, I had no symptoms. Maybe it was something I ate. Connie felt fine, so we ruled that out.

The hospital was only seven minutes away. At least this time I wasn't in an ambulance, so we laughed. The emergency room was quiet.

I explained my symptoms and history. They already had my records. I was immediately taken back ahead of everyone in the lobby. They put me on a bed and checked my vitals. My heart rate was elevated. My blood pressure was high—for me. A nurse came in and said they were drawing blood. She took the sample and left.

About an hour later, a doctor came in to talk to me. He said they wanted to do a scan. They were concerned about my heart but didn't elaborate. I was sent to the CT scan room and underwent a scan that lasted about thirty minutes. Afterward, they took me back to my room where Connie was waiting. We sat in relative silence. Questions were racing through our minds, but we didn't know what to say or ask.

The doctor returned and explained that my blood test results showed elevated troponins, which could indicate a coronary issue related to the damaged heart muscle from my cardiac arrest. They wanted to admit me and run more tests. Something wasn't right. Connie and I looked at each other. What was happening right now?

I was admitted to a room. IVs and heart monitors followed. The nurses were great, as usual. I was given something for nausea. I kept trying to understand how nausea and heart issues were connected, but no one really had an answer yet. They said the tests were to rule out problems. I was all for ruling out problems—I just didn't know what problems they meant.

Blood was drawn every four hours. I also had an echocardiogram. Most of the day was spent between blood tests, the echocardiogram, and another CT scan. It became clear I would be there a while. It was Friday, and the weekend was coming. By the end of the day, a doctor came in to speak with us.

The blood tests confirmed elevated troponins, a protein released when heart muscle is damaged. The echocardiogram showed the existing damage from before—significant damage to the lower left ventricle from the widow-maker I had sixteen months earlier. The question was why the protein levels were elevated now, and whether my symptoms pointed to something new happening with my heart.

The doctor ordered an angiogram for Saturday morning. At that point, we were full of questions. What could they possibly find? Was the test dangerous? He said it was a routine exploratory procedure to rule out any additional blockages.

Another blockage? I was already on major blood thinners. How could that be possible? He tried to reassure us, saying this was standard and precautionary.

My head was spinning. I immediately went into prayer.

"Dear God, what do You have in store for me now? I rejoice in Your mercy and grace. Please, God, let this pass from me."

Connie looked visibly worried. We were both in shock. Another echocardiogram and CT scan were done before morning. Connie went home to take care of Gibson.

She returned later for a short visit and brought my medications. She also brought me a vanilla shake. I felt deeply pensive about the sudden turn of events. Connie had called our kids and told them Dad was in the hospital again, but not to worry. She left around 8 p.m. and came back early the next morning.

My angiogram was scheduled for 7:30 a.m. They had to assemble a special team for the early Saturday procedure. I was awakened every four hours for blood draws. I didn't sleep at all. I watched TV, trying to keep my mind off the possible complications my heart could present. The doctor seemed unfazed by it all—so why should I worry?

I prayed all night.

I had learned many lessons. Give this to God. It is all part of His plan. He has never given me more than I could handle. The event on the stairs was still fresh in my mind. He had provided the phone call that led to financial help. I had been given new hips, and the pain was gone.

Every trial of my human condition had been resolved when I simply asked and trusted that He had me in His plans. It was His will, not mine.

Follow the light. Do not step back into the darkness.

He had shown me His light for my benefit. It was a true guiding light—one I prayed I would never stray from. I was worried, but I gave it to God. Morning was coming. I didn't know what it would bring, but I had faith in Him and the purpose He had for me.

One more blood draw, and then they came for me. I was wheeled down to the Cath Lab. The room was cold. They moved me onto another table. The space was filled with large machines, and a huge monitor was positioned near my head. They injected a dye into my IV, and I felt a hot sensation rush through my body, especially in my chest. I tried to stay cheerful with the nurses, who were very busy setting everything up.

One nurse seemed to be in charge. I whispered that I was sorry to bring her in so early on a Saturday morning. She laughed and said, "Don't worry, I'm making huge bucks!" That was exactly the humor I needed to break the tension.

The doctor came in and explained the procedure. I was given a type of sedation that didn't put me fully to sleep. I was in a twilight zone—not awake, but not asleep. I was able to watch the entire procedure on the monitor.

I lost track of time. The procedure lasted about four hours. The only thing I clearly remember was at the very end, when the doctor suddenly threw up her hands and pushed her chair back. In frustration, she said, "I'm done here. I can't get it."

What did that mean?

I was so sleepy that the next thing I remember was waking up in the recovery room. Connie was there, and she had a worried look on her face. I asked what they had found. She told me that both stents in my main artery were 100% blocked with a very hard substance.

The doctor came in to speak with us. She explained that she had gone through my artery with a catheter and found resistance in my main artery. She then inserted a wire through the catheter in an attempt to open the blockage inside the cage-like stents that were supposed to keep the artery open.

I was once again in trouble.

The only thing keeping me alive at that point was tiny collateral veins that had formed around the artery. These were the sole source of blood flow feeding the healthy portion of my heart.

One of my arteries—supplying the right side—had developed a solid blockage inside the stents. She could not penetrate it, no matter how hard she tried. Continuing to force it risked tearing the artery. She explained that the procedure was above her skill level and would require an exceptionally skilled specialist trained in a high-risk procedure called a Percutaneous Coronary Intervention, or PCI.

So who was this person, and where would we find them?

Three cardiologists all agreed on one doctor they felt was the smartest kid on the block. He was extremely busy, but they would try to arrange an immediate consultation. I spent the rest of the weekend in the hospital recovering from the extended procedure and under continued monitoring to be sure it was safe for me to go home. I was released on Monday to rest.

Once again, my human condition showed up. I prayed with rejoicing for the mercy and grace God had shown me. My heart had not failed, and I had survived yet again. No new hockey sticks for me. I still had work to do.

CHAPTER 17:
THE HUMAN CONDITION: FAITH IN ACTION

Imagine you are browsing in an old antique store and find a crystal ball. You hold it, and it magically allows you to see your future. If you knew you were going to be dead in your car in the next few hours, would you have that argument with your wife? Would you call those you haven't spoken to in a while? Would you make amends? What would go through your mind as this foreshadow of your death played out before you? If you could see the future, would you change the present?

Because there is no crystal ball of life, how do we know what to say or do? Like most people, I have encountered significant choices at various times in my life. Moments of clarity emerged when I made decisions based on unwavering principles, rather than making selections based on my own convenience. In contrast, times of darkness were the result of turning away from Christian principles and succumbing to my own will and desires. Every day of our lives we live in the human condition. This condition is the whole of every experience from birth to death, including the universal experiences we all share just from being human. The loss of a loved one unexpectedly. The possibility of lost employment coming out of left field. Did a seemingly minor health issue turn out to be a complete shock? The conditions we find ourselves in are often completely out of our control.

Do we chart our course based on the human instincts instilled in us from birth? Is it possible that when life happens, we simply do nothing and go about picking ourselves up and getting on with it? Or is there a larger purpose in our suffering? Is there a divine plan and design, driven by a creator?

Ask a person who has just lost everything if they would change anything. Sit and listen to someone who has just lost their child. They will tell you, "It's not supposed to be this way." Grief inherently involves second-guessing decisions: "I wish I would have paid attention…" "I should have reached out when I heard them suffering…" "What could I have said or done?" Their experience has defined the life-altering human condition I am describing. How does anyone make it through these terrible events? To survive the question of why requires tremendous faith—or existential tragedy will simply replace what it once was.

We endeavor to make it through our journey with survival at the minimum and success as the goal, whatever that may be to each of us. Are we ever truly defined by the success we strive to achieve? Do we overlook the things that really matter most? Are we really in charge of the outcomes of our lives? Our human condition raises many questions. Life's fast pace often blurs our surroundings.

I laugh sometimes when I see a dog with its head hanging out the window, tongue out, trying to taste and smell the world as it goes by at 65 miles per hour. But in truth, that is how we often live our own lives. I admit with humility that I had let life zoom past me. The music of life is not contained within the notes we are playing. Life really happens in the quiet space between the notes. Too often we rely on what is tangible. In music, the real magic happens when the silence between the notes is applied artistically. The pause in sound draws you to the next note. My life has been filled with noise that did not matter. I missed moments when just sitting still was all I really needed. I missed the signs of happiness and satisfaction because I was preoccupied with the noise of my own human condition.

Life itself is defined by its many events and experiences. Some bring us joy and happiness. Others remind us of how extremely difficult the human condition really is. We are constantly navigating through our years with the choices we think are before us. But what if our method of choosing is flawed? What happens when we find out, after all this time, we were wrong—as I did? When faced with death, are there regrets? I died to this world, only to be brought back. I was given a 1% chance to live life again.

I have often become entangled in the results of my perceived human condition. If I perceive myself as poor, I am. If I perceive myself as abundant, I am. What followed these perceptions were a cavalcade of achievements fomenting these truths I believed to be true. When I perceived that having massive numbers of friends made me valuable, I just looked at my follower count for validation. I would see myself as successful in business, and remind others of the watch I wear, the car I drive, and the home I live in. I believed I was religious, so I belonged to the most popular church.

The core principles of what I now try to live by are those that are truly set in stone. The human condition that will always be present is now an exercise in personal growth. I endeavor to face it with honesty, integrity, and faith. Nobody intentionally places a flagpole crooked in front of a monument. It is necessary to take time and measurements to ensure it is vertical. We place our honored flag on it, so we want to get it right for everyone to see. I have learned to measure my principles like a person setting a flagpole. I try to measure myself with a guide and rule that is true and honest. You cannot hide misalignment. Everyone sees it, even if you do not.

I either have integrity, or I do not. Integrity happens when others are not present most often. This is a principle I shoved aside when the pain of doing the right thing was overcome by my need to self-soothe. When called upon to do a task or simply lend a hand, I was not always there for the person completely.

Honesty really comes down to never telling yourself or others what they want to hear to affect an outcome. The real test is when asked for an opinion that could directly change the course of your own human condition. I am a realtor; the reward of closing on a home can at times be very lucrative. I don't sell anything; I serve. It is never good service to convince someone to buy so I can earn.

Empathy is the form of love you give for free, without any recognition or repayment. It takes a person of true character to genuinely care and be there for someone without judgment or conditions. You lose the empathy factor completely if you confuse their pain and suffering for lack of gratitude. You put out the effort for them yet expect them to reward you with the proper amount of gratitude. Where is the love in that?

Who do you call first in times of tragedy or devastating news? A family member who has always been there? A lifelong soulmate who never turned their back on you? Someone you invested in for 20 years, mentoring, who you can trust? We all need help from time to time. It's natural to ask someone we trust. But it's important to realize that our trusted friends and family all have their own human conditions to battle. Who do you call upon when they are not emotionally available? Do you despair in your loneliness? Or do you seek God?

True family and friends know when you are suffering and offer themselves. Hopefully, they are there for you without needing a reminder that you are not okay. To help is to do it freely, with love and empathy. Should I expect that the person in their worst condition would appear normal in their actions? If you have ever cared for a family member at the end stages of Alzheimer's, you know exactly how this feels. The simple moment they remember your name is enough.

I will share the incredible shame of wishing I could go back to where I was to escape my human condition. I hope to offer you the hope of knowing what lies beyond our mortal life. Many of my experiences left me with amazing revelations of the definition of a miracle. Some were extremely painful; this is the human condition. And while I believe it is not His will for us to suffer, I know He uses all situations for our good. Instant answers to prayer exist if I genuinely believe and accept His mercy.

We are all guilty of the worst behaviors when the human condition strikes. The choices we make that cause pain result from our misconceptions. We perceive it, so it is true. We act on our will alone. We get hurt or hurt others. This is the result of acting upon our own power to choose our free will. I have served my own purpose all my life. What have I learned through the struggles? Has the experience of being clinically dead and what I saw during the experience changed me? Absolutely.

Faith is a verb, not a noun. Faith is action. Faith is not something you have. Faith is something you do. I had to experience total failure, devastation, and intense pain to understand this. Through it all, I feel that acting in faith showed me my true self and God's purpose. I have discovered true faith through actively pursuing the answer.

I know that many reading this are curious about what it was like to experience death. Others are looking for evidence that life truly has meaning. This is for you—and only you—to decide. I can only relay the exact experience I had during and after I was brought back to this place called earth.

Consider the possibility that the extent of our human suffering is contingent on the amount of darkness we let ourselves fall into by our own accord. Is it possible that we are the sole party responsible for our own misery? Ask any billionaire if their life is void of difficulties. Keeping and maintaining over-the-top wealth has its share of disappointments and pitfalls. Is it possible that all the money in the world buys happiness? I think not.

I belong to the 1% club. I suffered a cardiac event and was clinically dead for approximately 20 minutes. Only 1% of people survive such an event. I am not supposed to be alive, let alone writing this book. This is the club everyone must die to be admitted to. Consider, hypothetically, how your life would be evaluated if you were on the other side, awake and cognizant. Would you look back with regrets? How many decisions would you rethink? Consider the obituary of your life as it is being read at your memorial. Would you beg for mercy and a second chance? Just maybe you would want to stay in the light forever.

Suddenly you return from a place where time stood still. A place so peaceful and majestic that you would never want to leave. You are told it is not your time, only to resume your human condition once again. The amazing view of the afterlife is seared in your memory. I hope you can glean from my experience a powerful and possibly devastating truth: you have a very finite time to get it right. You are not the timekeeper.

Life is fragile and can end in an instant. The human body is a complex marvel, coordinating multiple systems simultaneously to sustain life. I have abstained from drinking for 10 years and have maintained a high level of physical activity throughout my life. No matter how hard a person tries to keep their body moving, you can still find yourself dead in your car like I did. It is unimaginable what a shock it was to wake up in an intensive care unit with a tube in your throat.

Consider everything happening in your life right this very moment. For many, just surviving financially to the end of the month is all that matters, because another one is coming right after. Others are consumed with family and the day-to-day navigation of supporting a household, paying bills, feeding children, and solving just about every problem under the sun. Perhaps you manage a large company with countless deadlines, quotas, and projects. Many times, our human condition causes us to miss the forest for the trees.

From a very early age, I was physically active. I swam competitively and loved playing tennis. In high school, I took both swimming and tennis. My robust love of hockey followed me throughout high school and continues to this day (more on that later). In my late teens and early twenties, I climbed ice and rock all over the Western Rockies and Tetons mountain ranges. All these life experiences taught me to never give up and to have the courage to do extraordinary things.

From my mountaineering experience, I learned to start with the courage and confidence that I would finish—anything short of that would likely mean peril. I had the honor of learning from world-class climbers. One important lesson struck me the first time I sat on top of the Grand Teton: half of the battle was reaching the top. The other half was getting down. My guide that trip stopped me at the summit and offered the most important advice I would ever receive:

"Know when you are in the moment of your greatness. Stop and take a permanent photo in your mind and commit it to memory. You likely may never be there again."

He was so right.

Besides mountaineering, swimming, tennis, and hockey, I also enjoy martial arts. I began studying Taekwondo in 1984, which led to a long career culminating in earning a 5th-degree Black Belt in 2000. Martial arts opened many avenues in my professional life. I learned how to lead through humility and strength. I've thrown several thousand people to the ground. My greatest pleasure has been seeing my students surpass me and achieve Master. Taekwondo is a very physical martial art, and it took a real toll on my body—I taught by demonstration, never by theory. I eventually reached a point where I was simply tired of the constant healing, and with great sadness, I concluded that chapter in 2002.

Beginning in 1985, I eventually reached the level of Advanced Tactical Law Enforcement firearms and defensive tactics instructor. This placed me among many elite patriots serving our country. I was proud to be accepted among them and honored to train everyone from police recruits to Navy SEALs and everyone in between. Physically, I was at my peak. I had reached the pinnacles of many journeys, but it also came with deep scars of reality. The horror of seeing a best friend's brains on a wall after a failed entry conducted by the very SWAT team he was on—the team I had been training that morning—forever changed my life. That day's events and the funeral remain seared in my heart. I faced mortality, yet not my own.

What happens if you suddenly become completely incapacitated? Without any warning, your life ends, but a miracle saves you. The dinner table of your life isn't just rearranged; the tablecloth of your entire world as you knew it is yanked away, and the fine dishes you have amassed are smashed on the ground like a failed magician's trick. Everything—and I mean everything—is destroyed. Yet you are granted a second chance. What do you do with it? You are never really the same again.

My first action was to rejoice in being alive. We had lost everything, yet I rejoiced. Our lives were radically destroyed as we knew them, yet I still rejoiced in a new plan. A perfect plan lay before us. Do I know what it is exactly? Of course not. Am I fearful of the dark? No—I have stood in an indescribable light. As strange as it may seem, I have discovered through faith alone that I am not afraid of the darkness anymore.

How silly it must sound for someone to tell another, at the crux of their miserable human condition, to rejoice in it. Is it absurd to tell someone stumbling in the dark to turn the light on? If a person is freezing while holding a warm coat, shouldn't they simply put the coat on? Have you ever been so immersed in your own pain and confusion that nothing you can muster up works? Yet I feel that part of my second chance is to challenge the idea of suffering as wholly negative, when in truth it can strengthen our convictions and deepen our understanding of the world—if only we allow it to.

CHAPTER 18:
A LIFETIME OF LOVE

My father once said to me, "Son, stay clear of redheads and don't teach them to hit." My mother was a redhead, and they were married just short of 49 years. My biological father left my mother after Christmas 1968, leaving her with two very young boys and no way to support them. There she was: a single mom with two children, working at a local Weight Watchers for less than $2.00 an hour. Her family and friends stepped in when her in-laws turned their backs on her. She was divorced soon after, in 1969, and struggled to provide for our small family through the spring of that year. A very close friend introduced her to a widower named Frank, whose wife had recently died after a prolonged battle with cancer. He had a son and an adopted daughter.

Their first date was to a game of Donkey Baseball—yes, all the players rode on donkeys as they played baseball. Apparently, this is where great romances are forged. Soon after, the three of us moved to Arizona to live in a home owned by my mother's sister. A fresh start was in order, and we packed up and moved. Arizona was hot.

During our stay in Arizona, my brother and I spent a week with a babysitter. Frank proposed, and they flew to Las Vegas, where they were married at the Wedding Chapel on August 23, 1969. Shortly after, he moved us back to Omaha, Nebraska. They were inseparable until the end. Frank became my father in every sense of the word, and my mother's heart was broken when she had to say goodbye to the man who had protected her and adopted her two boys. Dementia claimed him in 2018.

The day my father died, I experienced the meaning of true love. My mother cuddled him all night as he slowly slipped away. She sweetly said goodbye, placing her hand on his flag-draped body. Years later, I have come to understand my mother's rejoicing over my father through her own loneliness and sorrow—he was with God now.

I have worked with many men and women who have served our country. I have had the honor of training law enforcement and distinguished members of our military. When my father died, I was determined to give him a memorial worthy of a Marine. A close friend had connections with a vintage WWII aviation group that provided full honors, including five vintage warplanes, an Honor Guard, and a lone bagpipe player with the sweetest rendition of *Amazing Grace*. It was beautiful and fitting for one of Uncle Sam's Misguided Children.

During his memorial, I was struck by just how fortunate I was to have my wife, Connie, by my side and my mother on the other. Connie had battled and won a vicious Triple Negative breast cancer. Her suffering during that battle was immeasurable. I fell deeper in love with her with each passing day. I had been so lost during her illness, thinking I might lose her forever. There I was, holding my mother's hand as she said her final goodbye to her mate. Her sorrow was profound, and she would be alone for the remaining two years of her life.

I have been married to my beautiful wife, Connie, since 1993. Frank was right about one thing: I probably should not have taught her to hit. When we met, she was shy and unassuming. Her beautiful red hair tied up reminded me of Pebbles Flintstone. Little did I know I had just fallen in love with the only woman on the planet who could truly understand me. She is a lion tamer. I recently learned that all these years she had been giving me the "side eye"—I thought she was just looking at me funny.

I met her at my Taekwondo school, where her daughter and son were enrolled on a gift certificate from a friend. I talked her into joining the adult classes at night. Connie had extensive gymnastics experience and a surprisingly dominant presence in class. She resisted saying "Yes, sir," as is customary in traditional martial arts. Likely, this should have been my first clue to her bossy nature.

I could write an entire book about our extremely eventful life together. It is safe to say she gets me like no other person. We have shared a life of successes and failures. We have weathered countless periods when the average marriage might have dissolved. I was in a career that took me down many paths, and she accepted her place within my various roles with grace and unwavering support.

My beautiful Connie is intensely private. I know some passages in this book may challenge her boundaries, and we have talked about that often. I felt that maybe just one person would be touched by our story, so she agreed to share. I love her for supporting my vision and for her willingness to place her privacy aside.

Our first date was a blues festival in Prescott, Arizona, about an hour from Phoenix. I was going through a divorce, as she was. We were cautious but comfortable with each other. The festival was a delight, and I was thrilled at how much fun she had. The ride home was filled with conversation as we shared parts of our lives.

As we returned, the conversation turned to marriage. Both of us were ending our previous marriages, and the discussion was deep and honest. I felt something about her instantly. Looking back, I now know the Holy Spirit was moving in me in a way it would take decades to fully understand. She asked the most blunt and honest question: "What do you want from a wife?"

My response was immediate: "I want to marry a woman who would bury me someday." That's it—someone who would see me to the end of my days. I have always admired my parents; they made it through thick and thin. My father stepped up and adopted my brother and me. I wanted that. Nothing more, nothing less. Everything in between I could handle. I just wanted to grow old with someone who would love me as much as I would love them.

We married two days after my divorce. I was technically a single man for one day—she maintains I was too busy grocery shopping for the reception. Our lives quickly melded together. Connie became deeply involved in my martial arts business, teaching classes and applying her business acumen. She was a force to be reckoned with—a partner, my other half.

Where was the shy, unassuming little redhead I married? Well, I had just taught her to hit. My father might have had something there. I vowed to honor and protect her for the rest of her life, and this included the kids. They needed a father; their biological father had denied them, just as mine had denied my brother and me. I adopted both children as my own shortly after. I had a lot to learn, just as my father had—and I still do.

Sitting between Connie and my mother on this monumental day of loss, my first conversation about my idea of marriage with Connie on our first date pounded my heart into the ground. I couldn't hold back the tears. I had a sudden flashback of the exact moment Connie placed my hand on the newly formed lump in her breast seven and a half years earlier. I remembered the sinking fear of losing her forever. Breast cancer would soon be a constant reminder of both of our fragile human conditions. God had spared me the anguish my mom was now feeling. I gave praise for His grace and mercy given to this undeserving soul every day.

My father passed away from the grinding effects of dementia in 2018. He left my mother to live the remaining two years of her life surrounded by friends and loved ones. She was slowly fading into the bosom of Alzheimer's. Alzheimer's is a cruel disease, yet there are solid moments of amazing revelation if you take the time to sit and just listen to the prattled mind. I am grateful my mom always remembered me. To her last conscious moment, she always greeted me with her familiar "Woo Hoo!"

CHAPTER 19:
TOMORROW HAS JUST BEGUN

My mother lived in a nice assisted-living facility on land that had once belonged to her sister and brother-in-law's cotton farm. The developer who subdivided the land recreated the tiny Iowa farm community where she and her sister had grown up. It always felt like home to her. The land held the spirit of a family farm. She often spoke about her life as a little girl on the dairy farm my grandmother tried to manage with her children after the grandfather I never met suddenly died when my mom was thirteen.

I would visit her frequently for breakfast. We would sit together, and she would fill me in on all the latest news. Some days she was spot-on, other days I had to gently guide her through minor tasks her brain had simply forgotten. She was always more interested in my life than her own. My music was always important to her. I've been playing the guitar since I was seven, starting in the third grade at Catholic school.

I grew up loving music. I was never told to practice—my mom encouraged me to always play in front of people. My dad, not so much. I led the music at Mass until I was fifteen. Bluegrass music became an early passion. By age twelve, I found myself performing in front of a massive Bluegrass festival with a professional family band of neighbors I had grown up with. I suppose that's when I first caught the performance bug.

From 2001 onward, I spent nearly ten years playing lead guitar at a large non-denominational church. That chapter ended abruptly when Connie got sick, and I never stepped foot on a church stage again. I did continue writing and composing my own music, often spending twenty hours a week practicing and teaching. I played with fellow musicians I met along the way. One student I taught grew into an exceptional guitarist, and I always felt honored to share the stage with him, taking pride in his talents and whatever small part I played in his success.

The music I wrote seemed to flow naturally. I regularly shared it with a friend and mentor who, in many ways, became a teacher to me. He was working toward recording and producing music, and often helped iron out the rough spots in my songs, making them come alive. Most of my joy came from the time we spent together, on and off stage, making music. A tragic misunderstanding, however, struck when I was at my absolute worst in spirit and health, costing us the friendship. I will forever mourn that period in my life.

One riff lingered in my head, refusing to leave. I wrote and rewrote the chords, recorded and re-recorded the melodies. The song never left me. I kept it on my phone, listening to it constantly. One morning, as I waited for my mother to arrive at the breakfast table where she lived, I saw her coming down the hall in her pajamas and bathrobe. I asked why she was still in her pajamas. She said, "What's the hurry? Tomorrow has just begun!"

That was it—the title of the song: *Tomorrow Has Just Begun*! I finally had a purpose. I was determined to write this song for my mother, hoping to surprise her someday. The song took shape and meaning. I played it everywhere I could to capture a live feel. The chords and melody began to blend naturally. That original riff had finally found its form. The song consumed me. Little did I know, the song I wanted to write for her would be the last melody she would hear in this lifetime.

On February 10th, 2020, my mother fell ill. At first, we weren't sure what was happening, but it soon became clear she was failing. The hospice nurse gently motioned that her time was close. She lost consciousness, and for several days that followed, we sat with her and prayed. Her breathing changed from slow and deep to the harsh, unmistakable death rattle. I recognized this stage well—my dad had passed the same way just two years earlier.

Her condition slowly but steadily deteriorated, and our prayers turned into pleas for mercy. "Please, dear God, take her and let her once again be united with the love of her life." I spent time simply talking to her. Occasionally, she would accept a bit of moisture on a swab. The nurse would give her medicine to calm her, and my mom slowly began to slip away.

I arrived early in the morning on Tuesday, February 18th, 2020. My mother had become completely still, except for the shallow rattle of her breathing. Her hospice nurse sat patiently beside her. I said a prayer and held my mother's hand.

I remember looking up through tears and asking the nurse if my mother was gone. She told me her spirit had left, but her body wasn't ready yet. It wouldn't be long now, she reassured me. I've never missed someone so deeply while they were still present. I prayed she would be with me once more, just for a single moment.

It was then that I felt a stirring in my heart. A sudden peace filled me. The room felt different. It was as if God spoke to me: *Play her song for her.* I placed my phone on the pillow beside her lifeless body, and the music quietly began. The melody moved through the room, and the music I had worked on—yet hadn't finished—seemed to speak to her soul. The nurse and I were both in tears.

The music carried through the chorus, and as the final notes came to an end, my mother smiled—her last smile on earth. As the nurse is my witness before God, that moment was real. She passed a short time later.

Isaiah 40:31 says:

> **"But they who wait on the Lord shall renew their strength; they shall mount up with wings like eagles; they shall run and not be weary; they shall walk and not faint."**

In the devastation of that loss, I came to understand that God's hand in my life moves on His timeline, not mine. When my strength runs out, I don't have to be finished. When I lean into God instead of my own force or urgency, I find a strength that carries me through what I could never carry on my own.

The COVID-19 pandemic struck exactly one month later. My mom was loved by so many. She had been the welcome ambassador at her assisted-living facility—everyone's friend. She had the Iowa gift of gab, which I'm sure is where I got mine. We had planned a memorial service at a lovely facility with a country farm feel. My mother had asked to be cremated, and the service was intended to allow family and friends from across the country to gather.

But it was March 15th, 2020. The governor placed the entire state under quarantine. Mass gatherings were prohibited as officials tried to understand what was happening. Elderly residents weren't even allowed to leave the facility to attend her service.

We held her beautiful memorial with only a few family members who were in town. Hundreds of her friends attended via telephone video. How tragic—a woman who touched so many lives remembered through a phone call. It was unbearably sad for me. I now had to face life without my parents. Generations change guard, and I realized I was now the next in line someday.

Connie was with me through every moment of grief. She knew when to give me space. Her words were exactly right when I needed comfort. She is always there—in good times and in sorrow.

CHAPTER 20:
A MOUNTAIN OF MUSIC TO CLIMB

The pandemic droned on. It felt like our country had been turned upside down. You know exactly where you were and what you had to do during those uncertain times. I was able to continue selling real estate as needed, and for that, I am thankful. I spent much of my spare time immersed in my music, determined to finish the song I had written for my mom. Hours upon hours went into refining it.

Eventually, the song made it to the recording studio. During that time, groups of people were still discouraged from gathering, especially in a studio setting. Recording this song became my Mount Everest—my ultimate musical achievement. How unbelievably difficult it was to record when other players couldn't be present. The process took far longer than I expected. Then, right in the middle of production, I took a fall and thought I had broken my right shoulder.

I didn't break it. What I had was massive arthritis from years of punishing my body. Soon, I would be the proud owner of a complete artificial shoulder implant. Dear God—what did this mean for my song? I could not lift my arm, let alone play the guitar. How long would recovery take? Would it feel different? The human condition had arrived in full force. My prayers shifted to healing. I asked God to make me whole again. The operation frightened me considerably.

As always, Connie was there to help me. The day after my replacement, I had an absolute panic attack, worried that my arm would somehow fall off. The anesthesia and pain medication were wearing off, and the reality of recovery set in. Rehab was just ahead, but for the following weeks, my thoughts were consumed by my song.

I was determined to strap my guitar back on and continue. Slowly, I returned to my home studio, putting in painful hours of strumming and picking to regain my playing strength. The first day back in the main studio was a major milestone. God had heard my prayers—He wanted me to finish this piece. I picked up right where I had left off.

This was the real deal. I was putting the song to rest. My friend committed to seeing the recording through to the end. He was monumental in adding the final touches, encouraging me to pull from my soul and play it for my mom. He poured love into the master recording. Once complete, he sent it to Burbank, California, to be mastered and published by one of the industry leaders in the field.

I cannot believe it—the song that made my mother smile would soon be mastered and published alongside other professional artists. Her last smile was now on every platform for the world to hear and enjoy. *Tomorrow Has Just Begun* is now available on the major music services. I am officially published. I climbed the hardest musical mountain of my lifetime. She would be so proud. After 52 years of playing music, I can now say my music lives on for everyone to enjoy. I hope you will find it and feel, for yourself, what love truly feels like.

CHAPTER 21:
THE WELD THAT BINDS US

I have spent over half of my life with Connie. She has never left my side. I have never met a more powerful and loving woman. I am so blessed to hold her hand every night as we lie in bed. Even during times of stress and tension, when we are working out our feelings, we have never eaten each other alive or denied our love and commitment. Connie has been a constant in my life. Without her, I would be lost.

It is a testimony to her presence in my life that she was the first name I screamed out when I was revived. She has been the soft voice of reason when I was unreasonable and a force to be reckoned with if I ever challenged her principles. Connie has carried her weight through the often-difficult human condition like an ant—small in stature, yet carrying a thousand times her load. Our children and grandchildren may never fully appreciate the depth of her love, as it has been a constant in our marriage. They know nothing else.

I could write volumes about our relationship. From the very beginning, we have experienced successes followed by failures. Our life has been full of hope, burdened with disaster. We have picked up the lead for one another as we each stood at death's door. Both of us know the fragility of each other's human condition. We can each recount what it feels like to be unconditionally loved while intimately experiencing each other's potential last moments. It is a profound gift from God—the gift of patient and faithful love for one another.

We share each day with the experiential knowledge that it could be our last. We have seen that potential up close and personal. This experience is not for the faint-hearted. The amount of stress and uncertainty we have endured could break most marriages, yet here we are, still holding hands. I am constantly reminded of my own parents at the end of their long and difficult life together holding each other close even as the other slipped away. My mom comforted my father, tearfully telling him it was okay to go. I am so blessed to know, with absolute certainty, that someday this will be our final chapter as well.

How does one define the perfect marriage without God at its center? I don't really have a clear answer. For some, it is the trophy wife, two kids, and a dog. For others, it may be a partner to share adventures with. Some see marriage as a trap, always looking for the nearest exit. How sad it must be to live in a self-imposed prison without a chance for parole.

Faith in the life God has given us created the weave of our lives together. This has ensured that our marriage is not a prison but a freedom in which we share the burdens of the human condition. We were two starving trees God planted next to each other by design. Our roots have melded so tightly together that our lives depend on each other for sustenance. It is our faith in God that allows us to survive all the trials life has to offer. Each challenge has led to a miracle. Each failure has led to hope. Nothing is easy for us—not even faith itself—but it is this faith that has allowed us to endure.

We laugh at the idea of winning the lottery. Neither of us feels God meant us to be filthy rich. We simply march on with faith. Prayer is our stronghold. Our prayers are answered when we seek His grace and mercy. We are both abundantly blessed and often marvel at how fortunate we are to have found one another. We agree that marriage is not for the weak of heart—it is often filled with difficulty and frustration.

Connie and I have been blessed with two incredible grandsons, just a little over a year and a half apart, who bring us immeasurable joy. My daughter and our first grandson lived with us in our home since 2013. Our second grandson arrived shortly after in 2015. Life became wonderfully busy as my daughter worked full-time, and the boys became part of our daily lives. Both

Connie and I found renewed purpose in this little family.

Waking up every morning and watching cartoons with toddlers became routine. Sharing their "firsts" was a gift—first day of kindergarten, first steps, first words. Having two young boys and our daughter living with us was an irreplaceable experience. It transformed our relationship and gave it profound meaning. I will forever be grateful to experience their growth from birth, a chance I had missed in my own life. Connie, of course, had already experienced her loss of a son in the seventh month of her pregnancy, named Dylan.

This little family has given us countless memories most grandparents never get to experience. The boys have become the central joy and purpose of our lives. From the very beginning, we have been locked in love with them. My daughter works tirelessly to raise them into fine young men, and Connie and I are always there to support her.

We were blessed to have them live with us for five years, giving my daughter time to purchase her first home and provide a proper place for them to grow. The boys continued to spend time with us, and I was able to relive my love of hockey vicariously through them.

Our testimony is one of patience and belief in one another. Recently, while enjoying dinner at our favorite pizza place, we agreed on one immutable truth about our marriage: we have both experienced each other on the very doorstep of death, literally.

CHAPTER 22:
ARE YOU MAD AT ME, OR WHAT?

It was September 9th, 2011. I returned home from work, and it was hot—I wanted to cool off in the pool. Connie had been distant for a couple of days. Sometimes, if I did or said something foolish, she would give me the cold shoulder. I had felt it and wanted to find out what I had done so we could reconnect.

We decided to have a beer and get into the pool. The afternoon sun cast shade on the water, and it felt good. She was still quiet, so I finally asked if I had upset her. For a couple of days, she hadn't really spoken to me. We were sitting on the steps when she simply placed my hand on the lower crease of her right breast. I knew immediately, though dread made my mind question it. "Is this what it feels like? Please God, no—it can't be." We just looked at each other for a moment.

It was like a bolt of lightning had struck between us. I felt a hard bump, about the size of a large pea.

At the time, we were showing Arabian horses. The owner of the stables, who had just recovered from thyroid cancer, was the first person I thought to ask for advice. While Connie was riding the next day, I told her about the lump. She scribbled the phone number of a radiologist on a post-it note and told me to call immediately.

We got in right away. It took two biopsies to reach the core of the lump—it was hard as a walnut. The radiologist didn't accept insurance, but a $15,000 check guaranteed immediate results. We would know the outcome the next day.

The next 24 hours were agonizing. Connie had just seen a show about a woman with Triple Negative Breast Cancer. At the time, she said she had felt overwhelming pity for the woman. Little did we know, Connie herself had Triple Negative, Stage 1, Grade 2 breast cancer—recently formed but aggressive.

We just held each other. She was petrified, and I was petrified for her. The radiologist had a team of doctors who would assemble and provide a prognosis. We were to meet the following week for their findings. The wait was excruciating. One thing we learned quickly: stay off the internet. Searching for her diagnosis online only amplified our fear.

At our appointment, we were given two options. Option one: radiation on the lump, followed by a lumpectomy and radical chemotherapy. Option two: a complete bilateral mastectomy, removal of a few sentinel nodes to check for cancer cells, followed by chemotherapy. They could also implant artificial breasts at the same time. There was no room for my input—this was her deeply personal decision. Connie chose the latter. How could she have known that this procedure, and the subsequent implants, would almost kill her three times?

On October 11th, 2011, Connie spent nine hours in surgery, having both breasts removed and two implants inserted. She made it through, but the pain was excruciating. Drains had been placed on both sides that required constant attention. She went home a couple of days later, only to return ten days later for surgery to have the implants scrubbed and irrigated—they were being rejected.

She was sent home again with strong antibiotics and pain medication. Ten days later, she returned with sepsis—an infection of the blood. The implants had to come out. This marked the beginning of the longest, most grueling fight I have ever witnessed. She had several close calls. God was not through with her yet.

I watched her melt away before my eyes from the harsh effects of chemo and a dozen surgeries. It was an enormous challenge to my faith to see her so sick. The human condition hit hard. How could God be in charge? Why her? I turned to Him and was reminded that He is always in control. All I had to do was accept the love He wanted to share with me.

I learned from her suffering that I had a choice. I could dwell in darkness, despairing the thought of losing her, or I could accept His grace and mercy for her and trust Him. My job was to be her husband in sickness and in health. I released her to God's care. He never fails; she was not done. She was not alone, and I could not leave her side. Several months of draining drains, administering medicine, and enduring surgeries were ahead. Neither of us knew what the future would hold.

Connie is beautiful in so many ways. Her face was angelic as she slept, a stocking cap covering her bald head. She was weak and vulnerable, yet so brave. At one point, while coaxing her to eat a bit of food, I joked that I was Nurse Nightingale. In her serious voice, she called me "Nurse Meany Gale." I admit, I am more drill sergeant than nurse. Over time, our roles would reverse.

That was Connie—the fighter, the conqueror. Her sarcasm returned. The get-up-and-go girl I loved was back. God's promise of restoration had begun. He was with her. I, as her husband, was there to do my part. I have never known this kind of love for anyone. Her suffering and bravery left me in awe. Her recovery was hard-fought and victorious.

"God is in the midst of her, she shall not be moved; God shall help her, just at the break of dawn." – Psalm 46:5

CHAPTER 23:
THE COMEBACK

In February of 2013, Connie was alive and vibrant once again. Her horse had missed her. During the tough days of chemotherapy, I had to drag her out of bed to visit her beautiful mare, Tristan. Tristan became a focal point of her progress.

For a few months, Connie was bald and wore a half wig with a do-rag. I found a place that had a prosthesis for her, helping cover up the fact that she was still in the process of rebuilding what cancer had taken. It was refreshing to be able to go out for a meal or just visit the horses.

Her first ride on Tristan brought us all to tears. What a beautiful sight it was to see her up on that horse, wig and all. The trainer was very nervous—Connie was still weak and unsure of herself—but seeing her flowing with Tristan once again somehow made the past few months blur. She had faced her fear head-on. Goliath was on the ground.

God is so good! My heart was soaring. She was back where she belonged. The year off had allowed the trainer to completely school her horse, and Tristan was ready to show off. She was about to compete in her next big show in Flagstaff. Little did we know it would almost be her last.

During warm-up in the outdoor arena, Tristan got spooked by a truck driving by. Connie was thrown from the horse with a foot still in the stirrup. The trainer quickly grabbed her foot and freed her. I had her in my arms, ready for the worst. The horse ran off, and the arena full of riders rushed to catch Tristan.

Connie was thoroughly embarrassed, covered in arena dirt from head to toe in her show clothes. Her face looked like a chimney sweep when she looked up at me, gray dirt streaking her cheeks. Mind you, I had just been through thick and thin with this woman. I told her she didn't have to do this—that it was okay to sit this one out.

True to form, she said, "Where's my #$%&ing horse?!" I pulled the horse's snot rag out of my pocket and wiped the dirt from her face. We all thought she was out of her mind to get back on. The trainer walked her and the horse to the show arena to wait for her class.

I must admit, I was nervous. I didn't want to spend any more time in the emergency room at this point. Would Tristan blow up again? Would Connie overreact and cause a train wreck? Arabian horses are notorious head cases.

We could not believe our eyes. Tristan went through the gates with the rest of the class and absolutely blew everyone away. It was as if the arena had sprinkled magic over her horse. Tristan lowered her head, found her position, and carried Connie through the class like they had been riding together nonstop for years. Connie barely had to do anything—she just sat there. She was beautiful, and I was in tears. She was back. Her goals accomplished, we sold Tristan that weekend. It was bittersweet, but it was time to move on.

What a journey, praise God! Connie had come from the bowels of cancer to the peak of the most majestic mountain. She was a vision of strength for all who knew her. Her battle was epic. Not only had she survived, but she had conquered. She was the definition of winning through adversity. Ladies looked up to her, respected her courage, and some even got checkups because of her example. One friend found her cancer early thanks to Connie's influence—she survived, just as Connie did.

Cancer is a cruel master. It is a thief. It will steal your identity and force you to bow down. It has no prejudice. No matter your race, creed, or economic status, cancer demands obedience, and no one is immune. It humbles the proud and defeats even the strongest warrior. Often, the cure is death. This is a facet of the human condition that knows no boundary—a river of death that meanders where it will.

However, one fact remains true: whether you live or die, God sees you through it. Whether in this life or the next, God reigns over this disease. Lift your eyes and seek His eternal love, and you will find peace through it all. Watching someone you deeply love endure this grind without faith is not for the faint of heart. The helplessness is indescribable. If you know, you know.

I have often met others who fought cancer or were caregivers to someone who did. Each person had their own perspective. Some never looked back and simply moved on. Others were left with the devastating loss of a loved one. In every case, cancer left an indelible mark on the soul. Mortality inevitably comes into view, and the question of what happens next lingers.

CHAPTER 24:
THEY CALL ME MOSES

It was late 2021, and our country was still reeling from the Covid-19 scare. Connie and I had yet to accept the need for any type of vaccine. However, we were very mindful of her cancer history and the potential lasting effects of the two rounds of chemotherapy she had undergone. Anyone who has faced—or watched a loved one face—chemotherapy knows what a terrible experience it can be. We both tried to put the past behind us and move on, but the reality remained: was she vulnerable to this unknown disease that had everyone in such an uproar? Both of our children worked in the medical field and were against taking any vaccines.

I regret my decision, but I decided to take the mRNA vaccine. My first shot was in October, and the second followed six weeks later. I did okay with the first shot, but the second had me thinking about the emergency room. I honestly thought I was going to have a heart attack and die. My entire body hurt. I had a very high fever and was overall terribly ill for approximately 24 hours—then I felt better. This was just after Thanksgiving 2021.

Fast forward to January 2022: I caught Covid-19. At the time, people were pouring across our southern border unchecked, and a new strain called Omicron hit Arizona like a hurricane. People were waiting in line for hours to be tested. I was so sick that I didn't need a doctor to tell me what I had. There was nothing to do but take Tylenol and rest in bed. Of course, I gave it to Connie. She got a sniffle and a slight temperature for a few days. I got the full boat. I looked up the symptoms—there were 18—and I had every single one.

I quarantined myself for two weeks and eventually began to feel better. I am very healthy as a rule. I do not drink or smoke. My resting heart rate is normally around 45–50, and my blood pressure is a lasting gift from my mother—usually around 96/70. I have always been healthy and efficient with regards to my cardiovascular health. I had been playing ice hockey a few times a week for fun right up to the point when I got sick.

After a couple of weeks, I was feeling better and ready to be in public again. I made an appointment with the only doctor I've seen in the past 15 years, just to be sure I was okay to be around people. We met, and she took a blood test, assuring me that I did indeed have Covid-19 but was at the tail end and unlikely to be contagious. My blood test results came back with enough antibodies to save an elephant.

I was finished being sick. I asked her if I could go back to playing hockey. She said, "Go be you." So, I went back to work and started playing again. My stamina was limited, and I was tired all the time. Sitting in open houses, I could barely stay awake. The virus had hit me hard. When I tried skating right away, I found myself gasping for air the first few times back.

I like to go play pickup hockey at a rink just a couple of miles from our home. Generally, the games start at noon and last about 90 minutes. I've played all my life and had recently started back after having my right shoulder replaced with an implant in late 2020. I didn't want to commit to a regular team due to time constraints and physical limitations with my shoulder. I wasn't quite ready for the big leagues.

The guys I found to play with range in skill from beginners to junior-level 20-year-olds getting ready for tryouts. The pace is fast but not too rough. It suited me fine, as I wasn't ready to be checked and risk my new shoulder. I'm still in pretty good shape and could mostly keep up. I was almost 60 at the time. I overheard a couple of the guys in the locker room saying they were '02 and the others said '04.

Curious about the numbers, I asked them what they meant. They said it was the year they were born and how they were placed on team rosters growing up. I said, "Oh, I'm a '62." I cracked up as one of them worked out the math in his head. They both smiled and said I was older than their dads. I said, "Just call me Moses." They laughed—and the name stuck. From that point on, I was Moses.

Ice hockey brings me back to my youth every time I step on the ice. It's hard to describe the wonderful sound of skates crunching across a quiet rink. The slap of my stick against the hard rubber puck is as contagious as anything I've ever experienced. The rink always has a very specific smell—a bit musty, a bit locker room. The constant drone of the ice compressors combined with the hum of the Zamboni resurfacing the ice is embedded in my soul.

I've played hockey in countless ice rinks. They were all quite similar—except for one: my home rink growing up. It's gone now, but the memories remain. I learned to skate on the frozen pond outside when I was six. The winter days were bitterly cold, but that didn't matter. Back then, hockey equipment was only for the big kids. We'd grind the toe picks of figure skates and tape Life magazines around our shins.

It cost fifty cents to skate in the indoor rink. Spending all day on a Saturday skating was the staple of life during Midwest winters. As I grew older, I became a "rink rat." We got free admission if we swept the lobby. The older boys would sweep and scrape the edges of the ice before the Zamboni came out to make it smooth as glass. I eventually progressed from rink rat to ice rink manager and Zamboni driver, holding that position for a year after high school.

I still love ice hockey. My son plays, and both of my young grandsons play as well. My pride and joy is a picture of the four of us on the ice together. Three generations of hockey players is a rare thing to see on the ice at once. Every chance I could get to slap a puck around with any of them was treasured. I wanted to create the same memories and love of the game that I had.

Ice hockey has become a connection to my youth. It's also a measure of my age—I'm not as fast as I used to be, and I stay clear of the boards for sure. But my love of the game has only grown. Little did I know that ice hockey would soon become a measure of my fight for survival. It would define my motivation to return to life as I know it. As time passes, I find myself more often the observer in the bleachers and the guy in the locker room tying skates for my grandsons.

I am repairing myself daily—mentally and physically. The road I've been on since the event that changed everything has been long and arduous. Many changes have occurred—some additions, many deletions in my normal way of living. To be sure, my human condition is still a daily wake-up call. One thing is certain: I am no longer driving the bus. I am the map holder now. God is in charge.

CHAPTER 25:
WHAT EXACTLY IS A TCO LAD PSI?

While my faith had begun to reshape how I saw my second chance at life, my body still had unfinished battles to fight. An appointment was made to meet with the cardiac specialist. He was a very introverted man with little to say, but he came highly regarded as the top specialist in Phoenix. He had extensive training in coronary interventions. Still, we had to pull answers out of him.

What exactly is the procedure? How long would it take? What were the risks? What degree of success should I expect?

Our minds were already overloaded. Of course, I Googled the procedure—and immediately regretted it. The potential for catastrophic outcomes was very real. Complications listed included a perforated artery, cardiac arrest, punctured heart muscle, kidney damage, stroke, and death—some of the very first items mentioned. The risk of complications ranged from 5% to 25%. It was one of the most nerve-wracking conversations I have ever had.

He explained that he would inject a radioactive dye into my arteries and insert two catheters, guided by X-ray—one through each femoral artery. From there, he would attempt to reach my main artery using a wire in each hand. Once there, he would try to open the stent with a balloon to widen the artery and remove the blockage. As with the angiogram, I would be awake.

Tests were ordered, and the procedure would be scheduled once the results came back. I was scheduled for a Total Occluded Left Anterior Descending Percutaneous Coronary Intervention—an absolute mouthful—on August 17th at 1:30 p.m. The procedure was expected to take six to eight hours. I was to arrive two hours early for pre-op. The waiting time was filled with the darkest thoughts.

I tried desperately not to think about the procedure. I suppose if I had felt some warmth or reassurance from the doctor, it might have helped. Instead, I retreated inward, focusing again on the light in my mind.

Was I going to die this time? Would something terrible happen? What about a stroke?

Every possible scenario played out in my head. I wrote a final note and placed it in my guitar case with instructions about the music I had written. I was deep into self-pity.

I prayed like I was about to die. This was PTSD surfacing again. I couldn't stop focusing on the risks. My mind completely blocked out the lower odds of failure. All I could think was, "What if?"

I had been through so many ups and downs that I didn't realize how mentally exhausted I had become. Who would have thought that being saved from a tragic death in my car would eventually lead here?

Connie did everything she could to stay optimistic. I was a tough case for her. She would often shut down my fear by focusing on good news from the day. Without her endless support and strength, I wouldn't have made it through. She was worried, but she carried an optimism I couldn't summon. My emotions were all over the place—grateful one moment, defeated the next. I never stopped praying for relief.

The days dragged on. "Get this thing out of my heart," I kept thinking. I was anxious and impatient at the same time. A very close friend I'd known since I was three years old, a cardiac nurse, became an invaluable source of support. She explained things in plain language and helped keep me from spiraling completely. Still, I was a wreck. Soon, the day arrived.

I woke up on the morning of the procedure feeling unusually hungry. Of course, I wasn't allowed to eat or drink, which only put me in a mood. I was quiet and pensive as Connie and I drove to the hospital. We didn't talk much. I checked in, and soon after, they took me back to pre-op.

I kissed Connie and told her how much I loved her. Valentine's morning crept into my mind—the memory of us parting after a fight without saying "I love you." I said a deep prayer in pre-op, giving everything to the Lord. I prayed for the surgeon's hands to be guided by God.

"Dear God, please send an angel into that room to watch over us all as they try to do this safely. Whatever the outcome, I will continue to praise You."

They took me to the Cath Lab once again. The room was filled with busy people in gowns and surgical gear. The atmosphere was serious and subdued. I sensed a very different energy this time. The doctor entered, greeting me briefly as he gave instructions and made adjustments. An anesthesiologist stood beside me, tasked with administering the radioactive dye and maintaining twilight sedation throughout the procedure.

Again, the hot sensation rushed through my body as the dye entered. The doctor made two firm punctures—one in each femoral artery. It was extremely uncomfortable. He was stern and insisted that I remain completely still. Soon enough, I was watching the monitor again.

I could feel pressure as the doctor pushed on both of my inner thighs. It felt like a long time of constant pressure before the wire finally appeared on the screen.

I watched the wire move slowly in and out of the vein. Sometimes it disappeared entirely, only to reappear moments later. The movements were deliberate and slow. The doctor would occasionally call out a number or a direction, then fall silent again. At times, I felt a tug or pressure in my chest. I would tell him, he'd call out another number, and the sensation would stop.

This went on for hours.

Occasionally, anxiety would build, and again he would call out a number, and it would ease. The thumping on my leg grew more noticeable—he was slapping my inner thigh repeatedly as I watched the wire on the screen.

Then suddenly, I felt a sharp pain in my chest. On the monitor, it looked like a drop of dye hitting water. I said, "Ouch—that hurts."

At that moment, he pushed away and said, "We're done here."

He had punctured a small hole in the artery. The procedure was over. The entire day was a failure.

I was in recovery and asleep when I woke to Connie standing beside me, disappointment written all over her face. The doctor came in shortly afterward. He was his usual introverted self, offering very few answers unless we pulled them out of him.

"What happened?" we asked.

Sometime near the end of the procedure, he had taken a wrong turn. The catheter had somehow ended up in the wrong area, and once that happened, everything unraveled.

Regardless of how it occurred, the result was the same: the main artery feeding my lower ventricle was still 100% blocked. The entire procedure had been for nothing.

We asked if he was going to try again. He said we would have to wait a minimum of eight weeks for the dye to fully leave my system; otherwise, I would risk permanent kidney damage. It was agreed that we would try again after that waiting period. This time, he said, he had a detailed map of my arteries and knew exactly where to go.

Eight weeks came and went. I scheduled another appointment, which ended up being ten weeks out. Connie and I went in together, and he told us it was safe to schedule a second attempt. Three weeks later, we received the call. The procedure was scheduled just before Christmas.

Here we go again. Hurry up and wait.

I felt like I had a ticking time bomb in my chest. I desperately wanted that clot out of my heart. Beyond that, I couldn't stop thinking about the ongoing damage. What was happening to my heart with zero direct blood flow, relying only on those tiny collateral veins that had begun to rejuvenate? At what point would I suffer another widow maker? Where would it strike next?

I wanted normal back.

CHAPTER 26:
THE PASSENGER IN MY BACKSEAT

We were struggling financially again. A real estate transaction I had been counting on completely collapsed. It involved my very good musician friend—my best friend—the same man who had started a GoFundMe for me when I was at my lowest. His heart was genuine, and I had been in a terrible place both emotionally and physically.

But I could see the signs early on: the two parties involved were on very different pages. Misunderstandings piled up. Feelings were hurt. Everything fell apart. I remain heartbroken over the loss of that friendship. He is still very dear to me.

At the time, I truly believed God was providing for us once again while I waited for the next PCI. I believed the income from that deal would sustain us for a long time.

I was completely wrong.

It cost me one of the most important friendships of my life, and we were suddenly on the verge of losing our home. My human condition showed up again, loud and clear. The loss of that friendship cut deeply. Would I do or say things differently if I could? Of course. But it was too late. He was gone—forever.

It was one of the saddest seasons I have ever lived through. I haven't picked up a guitar since that day. Music left my heart.

Still, I prayed. Still, I rejoiced in God's mercy and grace.

We needed emergency measures just to survive. I decided to rent a Lyft car and try to earn money by driving. We were waiting—again—very patiently for the next PCI attempt. It was scheduled for December 11th, 2023.

Physically, I felt fine. My hips were doing great. But it was the worst time of year in the real estate market to spend every waking hour chasing buyers who likely wouldn't appear. My experience confirmed it. Unless you have deals already closing in the fall or through the holidays, it simply isn't going to happen.

When you're ready, the metaphor behind **"The Passenger in My Back Seat"** is already forming—fear, mortality, faith, and waiting all riding with you. We can make that land even harder without losing restraint.

I had sold our other car to make ends meet. I signed up to drive for Lyft, and they would rent me a car for $290.00 per week. They took the lease payment out of my fees first. It took four days just to cover the lease. After spending roughly $30.00 a day on gas, I was making about $30.00 a day. I wanted to find something more stable, like a UPS store, but nobody was hiring someone my age. I had never been unemployed before. Driving added to our daily income, but it was clearly not enough.

Daily I prayed, "Please, Lord, put someone in my back seat who needs to hear the miracle of your light." And every single day, God delivered someone. I was starting to practice my enthusiastic voice again. It was good for me in many ways to mingle and serve people from so many walks of life. I made it a rule to never work past 9:00 p.m. I was fine delivering people to bars, but I drew the line at picking them up.

I gave over 3,000 rides. Ninety-five percent of them were very positive. I had some truly interesting conversations, just asking people where they were from. I found it amazing to see the variety of personalities from different places across the globe—some friendly, others more reserved. I had zero tolerance for people who were disrespectful or mean. They quickly found themselves standing on a street corner looking for another ride.

I would always start with, *"How's your day?"* Sometimes it snapped people out of a bad mood. Other times they shared the tough times they were having. What a perspective I was gaining. I was going through the worst period of my life, yet I would pray for the person in my back seat to feel love from me. My life was crashing around me, but I prayed for their peace. God put me in this humble position for a reason. This time, I intended to follow His will and grow from it.

Every day, I would clean out my car and get ready to leave. The moment I put my seat belt on, I prayed for my daily blessing and safety. I always thanked God for another day and my beating heart. My prayer was not only for me but for the person He would put in my care. I had complete faith that every person I met was delivered to me for a reason. He never failed me. Hundreds of riders were reaffirmed in the existence and power of miracles. I shared my story a couple thousand times. Without fail, I would end by saying, "You were put in my back seat on purpose. You have just been blessed." I lost count of how many times I was parked at a rider's destination, praying with them in my back seat. Countless times, the person would leave my car hoping to ride with me again.

One example of God's hand at work was a particular Sunday. I said my daily prayer. The morning was typical—Sundays were usually trips to a restaurant or to and from the airport. The one thing that could cause consternation was when a rider ran past the time they were supposed to be ready. I know people can be late, but it put me in the position of waiting and spending time for free while they casually got ready.

This Sunday, I was waiting for a passenger outside his house. I could see him moving slowly around inside through the app. Barely moving at all. The timer ran out, and now it was my choice to leave or stay. I felt my patience beginning to thin. Just as I was about to grumble and hit cancel, God tapped me on the shoulder and reminded me of my prayer. I would wait for this person.

He took ten extra minutes to come out. I would have had another ride by then, but I waited.

The young man got into my car. No hello. No thank you for waiting. I asked him how his day was going. He grumbled, "Alright." There was a deep sadness in his voice. He was headed to the Phoenix airport, which meant I was about to spend thirty minutes with him.

I asked where he was flying to. He said Detroit. Making small talk, I asked if he was from Detroit. He said he had just moved to Arizona a few months earlier. He began to loosen up. I asked if he was going back to see family. Quietly, almost under his breath, he said, "My Mamaw is going to die. I might be too late though."

Bam. Right in the heart.

I took a quick breath because I was about to cry and rejoice at the same time. God had slowed my patience so this burdened soul would be delivered to me. By now, I had learned to recognize when the Holy Spirit spoke loudly. I asked him about his Mamaw. He said, "She raised me and my sister." I asked if she was a good cook. He smiled faintly and said she was the best.

In that moment, I knew this young man's heart completely. He wasn't afraid of death—he was afraid of missing goodbye.

I asked him if I could share my story. He said, "Sure." For the next ten minutes, I told him what happened to me—how I had died, how I had watched the entire scene from above, and how I had been surrounded by the most magnificent light. I took special care describing the peace, the warmth, and the overwhelming love. When I told him my mother had said, *"Not yet, not yet,"* I glanced at him in the rearview mirror. He was sobbing.

I told him it was time to rejoice.

Right there, in my back seat, it was time to rejoice for his Mamaw. She was about to meet her Heavenly Father and receive her eternal reward. I told him this was the moment to see God's powerful love for her.

We reached the airport exit. We still had about ten minutes together. His entire demeanor had changed. He was smiling—really smiling now. It was as if the Holy Spirit had him in the grip of revelation.

I said, "I prayed this morning that God would put someone in my back seat who needed to hear about His light. Your Mamaw is about to be in His glory, and she is speaking to you right now."

His face lit up. He laughed through tears, shaking his head. "I feel her right now. This is crazy. I feel her right now!"

We pulled up to the curb. We both got out and met at the trunk where his luggage was stored. I gave him a huge grandpa hug and gently held his face in my hands. Smiling, I said, "In all things rejoice. God is real. Miracles happen every day. And Heaven is indescribable."

We parted with a prayer. God is so good.

I continued driving through the Thanksgiving holiday. Connie and I would pass each other throughout the day like ships in the night. Nighttime was when we finally connected. We ate very modest meals and fell asleep watching TV. I had grown accustomed to being apart from her, but that was the hardest part—being away from each other. We shared our days the best we could. Most nights we were so exhausted it was dinner in bed and good night.

I drove right up until the day before my scheduled PCI. December 11th, 2023 arrived. We were to be at the hospital at 1:00 p.m., with the procedure scheduled for 3:00. It was planned to last six to eight hours, and I was ready for it to be over.

We arrived and checked in. Everything seemed to be going according to plan. I had my wristband on and was slowly wrapping my mind around what was about to happen. I prayed for success this time. Connie offered her usual optimism. I could tell she was trying to convince herself—just as much as me—that this would finally be the end of it.

With everything we had been through, this did hold some type of closure for us both. I was feeling cautiously optimistic. After all, the doctor had said he had mapped my arteries during the last attempt, so this time it would be easier. We reassured each other that most of our fears the last time had come from the unknown. Too much time on the internet had produced little tangible hope.

The truth of the matter was that I was a unique case. Nothing really made sense—to me or to the doctors. It had been four months since the last failed procedure. What had changed? Was my heart still as healthy as it had been before they found the clot in July? What damage might a completely blocked artery have done to my heart? I guess the next hours would tell the tale of success or failure. It was already 3:00 p.m. I should be called any moment now.

3:00 p.m. came and went. Then 4:00 p.m. Neither of us had any idea what was happening. I wanted to get the show on the road. There I sat, hospital wristband on, overnight bag packed, ready to go. I wanted to check in. Connie was trying to coax me to be patient.

By 4:30 p.m., still nothing. I went to the registration desk to ask if something had gone wrong. The lady behind the desk said that, as far as she knew, everything was okay and that sometimes these things happen.

By 5:00 p.m., it was clear—the procedure was not happening. On a Friday night, it would have ended after 10:00 p.m. Something had clearly gone wrong. I returned to the desk and asked her to check again. Ten minutes later, she called me back. The doctor wasn't going to make it. Something else had come up.

The level of disappointment was palpable. We drove home in frustration. What had just happened?

CHAPTER 27:
TOUGH CHOICES

On Monday, I called the specialist's office and requested a return call. Nothing. The entire week passed without a response. Had he simply forgotten about us? I called again to confirm my scheduled procedure. They said they hadn't seen him in any other case that day. Yes, he had been in town. Was there a miscommunication? Were we supposed to be ready at another time? Still nothing from the office staff. I had been ghosted by a doctor. In all my days, I have never seen anything like it.

I called multiple times. Silence was the best I got. What was going on? I called my cardiologist and got in the very next day. He had been my advocate from the moment he saved my life and recognized how rare my situation was. Side note for readers:

If you have a health issue, your doctor should be your advocate. Do not accept anything less. Life is far too short to be shortened by a doctor.

I cannot praise my cardiologist and his staff enough. He was concerned about the lack of communication and professionalism. I told him that I had been told the specialist had no other cases that day. He didn't double book procedures, he was in town, and he simply didn't show up. He promised to get to the bottom of it. Apparently, the specialist didn't show because he wanted the help of another doctor. Why didn't he just say so?

I fired the specialist on the spot. I asked my cardiologist to find a replacement. A senior doctor at another hospital was the only option. My cardiologist had studied under him and called in a favor. He asked the specialist to examine me and meet for a consultation.

Two months dwindled by. Connie and I were driving daily and slipping further into a financial hole. Our world was so far removed from the urgent issue of a complete blockage of my main artery. It was simply unbelievable what was happening to us.

Finally, I received a call from the office staff of the new specialist. My appointment was scheduled for mid-February 2024, the day after Valentine's Day. More waiting and seeing. I rejoiced in the Lord for the virtue of patience.

When we arrived at the new specialist's office, sitting in the waiting room was an entirely different scenario. I was surrounded by people who belonged there—obese individuals with clear heart issues, elderly patients accompanied by caregivers. Never before had I felt so out of place—a man who had just been skating and playing hockey with a bunch of juniors.

Yet here I was. Connie sat by my side, quietly waiting for my name to be called. When it was my turn, I was led into the examining room. We both sat there in silence, waiting for the doctor to arrive. A knock, a "hello," and in came the doctor, accompanied by a physician's assistant.

He was a tall man who spoke with confidence. He asked me a number of questions about myself, showing particular interest in the day of my cardiac arrest and the events leading up to it. I told him I had been playing hockey that day and quipped that I wanted to get better so I could get a new hockey stick. He was intrigued—not just that I was alive, but that I was a hockey player. He had read my full report and was impressed by how healthy I was, given the circumstances.

He took the time to review all the films from the initial angioplasty, the day of my cardiac arrest, and my PCI. He explained why the PCI had been such a difficult procedure. "Your artery," he said, "is like an upside-down licorice rope." The instruments had to be inserted from the femoral artery at the bottom, and just getting the wires in was a challenge. The clot was an entirely separate obstacle.

In my case, he said, attempting such a dangerous procedure to save the artery that fed the dead portion of my heart made little sense.

"Wait a minute! What?"

Yes. My heart muscle was 35% dead. The blocked artery no longer served any purpose. The collateral veins that had rejuvenated were supplying blood to the remaining live tissue.

He had spoken with the other specialist when my PCI films were requested. The other specialist simply wasn't up for the task. The new specialist said he had been asked to assist the doctor I fired. I expressed my concerns—I did not want a man to touch my body who had so quickly disregarded me without a simple follow-up. The new specialist understood and said he was willing to try but didn't feel it would be fruitful at this point.

I asked what I should do next. His answer was simple: "Go buy a hockey stick." Exercise was my best medicine. I needed to grow those collateral veins—they were literally keeping me alive.

The news that my heart would be permanently colluded did not sit well with me. I was diagnosed with Ischemic Cardiomyopathy, now at risk for an enlarged heart and congestive heart failure. I would likely be on heart medication for the rest of my life. Still, I rejoiced in the miracle of the life I had been afforded.

My heart outcome was uncertain; only time would tell. Meanwhile, Connie and I were falling desperately behind. We drove seven days a week, but it wasn't enough. It was time to start offloading our most precious possessions. I began with my musical equipment. Over 55 years of playing the guitar, I had acquired some fine instruments. Two guitars, in particular, had been with me for more than 50 years and were priceless.

God was about to teach us both a hard lesson in humility. I shifted away from my love of music and entered a mode of complete deference. Every time I sold an instrument, a piece of my life went with it. The Vintage Gibson

Les Paul—a cherished piece of art with a tone that had graced countless stages—was gone.

I sold my go-to Fender Standard Stratocaster to a young college student learning to play guitar. I had put roughly 10,000 hours into that guitar. It had been featured in my song honoring my mother, *"Tomorrow Has Just Begun."* A huge part of me was invested in that piece of wood.

Next was a beautiful cherry guitar—the instrument I used for teaching. I had been teaching music for 40 years. When that guitar left, my love of teaching felt crushed. I love sharing music, and now I felt empty inside. My sound system and personal amplifier were the last to go. After that, all I had left were a few microphones and miles of cable.

The studio I had spent thousands of hours in was returned to its original room. Next came my office. The solid desk where I had written hundreds of contracts—gone. Oh well, I could still use a laptop. I didn't need it anyway.

We needed to completely lighten our load. I once learned that the best travelers could go all day without placing their bags on the ground. So be careful what you must carry with you.

This was ringing in my head: God was delivering us our sustenance through humility and self-sacrifice. So be it—I would rejoice in the experience. Each difficult moment had brought me a profound sense of internal introspection. The life I knew was completely rearranged. Nothing was the same. Exceedingly difficult times lay ahead, and it was only through trust in God and in each other that we were able to keep our heads up.

It was time to clear out our storage unit. That alone was a major lesson about the baggage we carried with us. Some of those things had traveled with us in boxes for 25 years. It was time to let go of memories and embrace the reality we faced. Nobody was coming to save us; we had to be ready for the hard times ahead.

We sold off as much as anyone would buy from the storage unit. Next came our backyard furniture. We had loved sitting together in the yard, spending many nights in long conversations. Eventually, we found ourselves sitting daily in a McDonald's, having our morning coffee. We could adjust as long as we had each other. Hours were spent dreaming about how life would be better someday. We were humbled by our poverty, but it would never break us. We clung to each other through the worst of times.

One of the grimmest moments for me personally was selling the many beautiful pieces of jewelry I had bought or had made for Connie. I had so enjoyed spoiling her with shiny things, and now it was all gone. The final, most painful moment was pawning our wedding rings. She had worn her set since we were married in December 1993.

That diamond was special. I had arranged for it to be delivered to our table at the Grand El Tovar Hotel dining room at the Grand Canyon, next to the massive 90-year-old stone fireplace. We had eaten some questionable appetizers in Flagstaff on the way up, trying our best to be hungry. I wanted to make this night special. While she took a nap, I slipped the dining room manager a twenty-dollar bill to set the table just right. The diamond ring was to be delivered on the dessert tray.

We dressed up and made a formal night of it. Dinner was light, but we ate. The table was set apart from the other guests. As the waiter brought out the lazy Susan with dessert, I noticed the room's eyes on her. The whole room knew it was our honeymoon. She didn't take the bait—she wasn't hungry for dessert. Then the waiter turned to the plate holding a red velvet ring box, surrounded by flowers, containing her diamond ring. She thought it was some kind of joke.

By now, the room was smiling and giggling. She couldn't make sense of the ring at first, but then it hit her. She took the ring, put it on her finger, and lifted her hand so it caught the light. The entire room erupted in applause. The ring was gone, but the memory would forever remain in the depth of my heart.

My father was in his last moments on Earth. I was with him until the end. I closed his eyes after he passed and gently removed his wedding ring, giving it to my mother. With tears in her eyes, she handed me the ring he had worn for 49 and a half years. I wore that ring with the memories it represented. Now it was gone, forever. That hit me hard. Still, I rejoiced in the love God had for me. I turned to the light and trusted He had more for us.

The times we were going through are branded on my heart. Not so much for me, but for Connie. My health seemed to be failing me, and I felt a deep sense of having broken my promise to her. As much as I wanted to be strong for her, I was weak and frail. Exhausted from driving, I wasn't capable of much more. Just functioning was a struggle, let alone striving like I used to. I lacked stamina, always out of breath, and would take a 90-minute nap on a moment's notice.

I was searching for some sense of identity. I was too old to start over, and too young to quit living. Yet, I had become stronger than ever in my faith. I had learned to let go and accept God's will for me. I knew I had a purpose, but what was it? Where would this devastation lead me? As I write this, I remember the words my ghostwriter, Anna, said: "God has provided you with an incredible story to share. The world will be blessed through your trials, so you must deliver it."

She was right. I began sharing my miracle with others—passengers in my car, followers on social media, people on podcasts. They were moved by the story of my near-death experience. Yet I still needed closure, an ending to the strife, proof of the miracle. I had more to learn about God's will, not mine, before that could happen.

Have you ever been hit by your own human condition, watching it crumble around you? When you find yourself in the middle of a tornado, whether you caused it or not, does it knock you to your knees? Life's roller coaster can spin at breakneck speed, with jarring turns. I was at the point of breaking. What would you do differently if you were me? When would you give up—or press forward into the unknown wilderness? This saga had become too much to handle alone.

Perhaps the lesson for all of us is to rejoice every day. Sunshine or clouds, rejoice. God has been there with me 100% of the time. When you find yourself asking, *What's next?*, rejoice—because the best is yet to come. Listen to the Holy Spirit; the answer lies in the quiet whispers of His presence. For me, God needed a trumpet to deliver His message of salvation and love. I was too stubborn to hear anything but the loudness of my hardship, the pain my human condition produced.

I encourage anyone reading this to stop and listen. At first, it will be faint. Pour yourself into your soul, seek the light, and repent. Say you're sorry, ask God to forgive you, and seek Him. He has been with me the whole time. His love is ours to claim; we simply must ask of our own free will. I release my fears. I give Him the reins of my life and allow Him to chart my path. What is mine never truly was. He provides everything I need, and He will do the same for you if you step out of your own way.

At what point does the human condition stop interrupting peace and quiet? Likely never—at least not until we no longer need His help and guidance. For me, He was not finished molding me into the purpose He had planned. I still had a basket of pride to empty first. The rest of the path would become obvious. I had to learn to turn His light on—and keep it on—or I would continue tripping in my own darkness. Are you struggling in the dark?

CHAPTER 28:
EMPTY HOUSE, NEW BEGINNING

The boys continued to stay with us as often. It didn't seem to faze them that our house was disappearing around us. We were about to move out of the home we had lived in for years. We simply couldn't afford it anymore. We were on the verge of homelessness. Time was running out; eviction papers had been served. Despite it all, the landlord was understanding and gave us every consideration. It was time to move before we had no choice left.

We were allowed to stay with our daughter. It was not the ideal situation by any means. Her home was very busy, with two boys, my son, and his big, beautiful Great Dane also living there. She gave us the master bedroom and bathroom, sacrificing her own space for us. She was just getting her life together, and here we were under her roof. I was still very weak and unable to keep up with moving our belongings into storage.

I was trying hard to put together a resume at the time, hoping to present it to a new-build company where a very close friend worked. After all, I had vast experience in real estate, but I just couldn't gain traction in the resale market again. Perhaps a change of venue would help. We were living in my daughter's house, but I spent the remaining two weeks at our old home by myself in the mornings, typing and polishing my resume. Afternoons and early evenings were spent driving for Lyft.

Connie and I would meet up at the house to watch a movie on the computer, and sometimes we would just stay overnight, sleeping on the floor with the dog on blankets. We clung to the last morsels of privacy and togetherness before the inevitable eviction. We refused to let it break our love for each other, even under the weight of the rubble our lives had become. Perhaps some of you have been in a similar place, where the chaos of life threatens to consume everything you hold dear. We were determined it would not.

I had not written a resume in 35 years. Where do you even start? What should go in one? A dear friend helped me navigate the technology, while another friend, a sales manager at a builder, could only put it in front of the right people. The rest was up to me. I wrote and rewrote the story of my life—a painful reflection of what I used to be and what I had become. I prayed for God to guide my hand. Have you ever been forced to restart your life? Or are you at the very beginning of your adventure, with decades stretching ahead of you? Either way, the future is always uncertain.

I sent the final copy of my resume to my friend, the sales manager, and waited. A couple of weeks later, I was notified I was in line for a first interview. Out of 4,500 applicants, I had been selected for an online interview. The timing coincided with our final days at the house on July 8th, 2024. I conducted the interview from my daughter's bedroom. It was awkward. I had set up a virtual background on Zoom, but I still felt inadequate.

I discovered the name of the interviewer beforehand and researched him thoroughly. To the social media addicts out there, know that just a few keystrokes can reveal a lot. I learned where he was born, the name of his college lacrosse team, and that he had been hired right out of college with no prior experience selling homes.

I dressed professionally and put the dog outside. The interview lasted about an hour. Most of the questions were basic introductory types. I was twice his age and felt as if I were sitting at the little kid's table. The last job interview I had was 35 years ago, with a Brigadier General quizzing me for a security clearance. Yet here I was, applying to work for someone else. I hadn't worked for a company in 20 years. I knew I didn't always play well with others, and I wondered if I could embrace this company—and if they could embrace me. Only time would tell.

I concluded the interview with a few questions of my own. I thanked him for his time and signed off. He said I would be contacted by the end of July. I was still exhausted and returned to driving that afternoon, deep in thought about the interview for the entirety of my shift.

Was this a new beginning? The job paid benefits and withheld taxes—both concepts were new to me. I had been self-employed since I was 19. Working for an actual employer was an entirely new experience.

CHAPTER 29:
HERE I GO AGAIN

I was driving from morning straight through to evening now. I felt a strange sense of relief being at my daughter's home. Connie and I were having a difficult time settling in. The house was not big enough for all of us, and we were confined to the bedroom. We were vulnerable, sad, and feeling the stress of nearly being homeless. The situation was difficult for everyone involved. We tried to leave as little footprint as possible, but it was hard.

The grandboys were with us in our room constantly. They were adjusting to the different arrangements, accustomed to being at our house, now finding themselves here. I felt blessed and extremely thankful that our daughter had opened her home to us. She works long, grueling hours in hospice as a nurse, spending her days caring for others at the end of life. Coming home to a crowded house was difficult for her, and we would never forget her generosity or the time we spent there.

Summer hockey was in full swing. The youngest grandson had a game at 1:30 pm on Saturday at the local rink in Gilbert—where I used to play. Our daughter was on call and had a patient, so I needed to meet him at the rink, get him dressed, and tie his skates. I had been driving all morning, and it was exceptionally hot, about 116 degrees. Getting in and out of the car to help my riders required constant hydration.

I was finishing my last ride to his home and preparing to head to the rink. I felt a strange tightness in my neck and chest. As I neared the rink, I became short of breath. I met my grandson in the lobby, while my daughter went back to her car. We hurried to find his locker room. The rink was cool, as usual. I hurriedly helped him put on his gear—the skates always went on last.

As I tied his skates, I felt increasingly out of breath. We had to hurry to the other side of the rink. He was about to be late, so we ran. I got him on the ice just as the referee blew the whistle. I paused by the glass for a moment—it's always nice and cool there in the summer. Then I felt dizzy. I took a sip of water, but my ears began ringing, and I felt faint. Lightheaded.

My daughter noticed and asked how I felt. I told her I wasn't well. She said I looked pale and sat me down on the bleachers while retrieving her medical bag from the car. She handed me a cold glass bottle to place on my neck. I felt like I might pass out.

She returned from the car with some salt to swallow and checked my blood pressure and vitals. Everything seemed normal at the time. I told her I was feeling worse and needed to lie down somewhere. We walked to the lobby and found a bench. I remember sitting next to her.

Suddenly, I went unconscious and slumped onto her. Later, she explained that she had yelled for help. A couple of dads helped get me to the floor. She called 911, telling the operator that I had just slumped and was unresponsive. My pulse was weak, and my breathing very shallow. She was instructed to give a single chest compression, even though I had a pulse. I groaned but remained unconscious.

The fire department arrived and loaded me into the ambulance. My son, who works for another station, joined them. They welcomed him aboard. I was still unresponsive upon arrival at the ER—the same ER I had been to twice before. Semi-conscious, I couldn't move at all.

I was able to respond to commands but couldn't move my arms or legs. Panic set in: did I have a stroke? What was happening? Why couldn't I move? Much of the ER is a blur in my memory. They rushed me into the CT scan room. Several people were pressing metal instruments into the soles of my feet—I felt nothing. My elbows were tested the same way. They were deeply concerned. What had happened? What caused both sides of my body to be numb? Usually, a stroke affects only one side.

They put me into the scanner and took several pictures of my brain. I was scared and emotional. What was happening to me now? I prayed silently to fall asleep, and when I woke up, I was back in the ER room. Connie and my son were there. I still couldn't move anything. The hospital staff moved me to a room. "I'm going to be here for a while," I thought. Exhausted, I just shut my eyes and fell asleep.

When I woke up, Connie was sitting beside me. I asked her what had just happened. Had I had another heart attack? She said they didn't think so. Instead, they were focused on ruling out a stroke or possibly a blood flow issue to my brain. Slowly, I began to regain some feeling in my arms and legs, though I still had an unbelievably bad headache. The nursing staff, as amazing as always, gave me something to relieve it.

Over the following days, I underwent numerous tests. My heart was ruled out as the cause. They performed another scan and an MRI of my brain. No signs of a stroke, not even a TIA—a small, temporary stroke. Ultimately, I was released to rest at home. The cause remained a mystery. My cardiologist remained suspicious and ordered a complete MRI of my heart. We were weighing whether another attempt at the PCI might be worthwhile, or if the issue was possibly electrical in nature.

I had the MRI done and entered a waiting period for the results. It wasn't until the end of July that I got the results. My ejection fraction read 37%. This number measures the percentage of blood pumped out of the lower chamber of the heart with each beat. Too low. My cardiologist felt that attempting the PCI again would be far too risky, with the likelihood of failure still high. It was decided I would see a cardiologist specializing in the electrical systems of the heart.

The waiting continued. I felt unusually weak, and my heart rate would spike to 170 BPM with minimal effort. Mowing my daughter's small lawn nearly caused me to collapse. I prayed for answers and held fast to my faith, unsure what was coming next.

Amid all this uncertainty, I was called back for a face-to-face interview with the Regional Vice President of the builder I had applied to. The interview was scheduled in just four days—a very short notice considering everything I was experiencing. I shifted my focus toward this opportunity, which could change our financial trajectory. I attended the meeting and felt it went well. The location of the job was an hour away, one way.

Committing to a two-hour commute each day, plus 8–10-hour workdays, made me question if I had the energy to manage it all. Still, I rejoiced and let God take the wheel. If it was His will, it would happen; I relinquished all control of my destiny. I had learned that I needed to follow God's map for me. The path He laid out was filled with markers and directional signs. Like any long journey, I had to pay attention to the details.

The day of my appointment with yet another cardiologist arrived. Connie and I sat in the office, wondering what would come next. The doctor came in—a cheerful, talkative man. We immediately liked him. He went over the details of my last MRI and got right to the point: my heart was right on the verge of needing assistance with the pacing of its beats.

My ejection fraction was 37%. At 35%, a pacemaker and defibrillator were required. My heart sank. I knew what that meant, and I didn't want any of it—but I had no choice. The doctor explained he needed to perform an electrical profile of my heart. This test would reveal the heart's ability to regulate itself normally. With 35% of my lower ventricle scarred, it was possible that the electrical signals were already compromised.

He wouldn't be able to be sure until he put a catheter into my heart via the femoral artery. Once in place, he would chemically stress my heart, causing it to beat over 200 times per minute. Essentially, he was going to induce tachycardia—an out-of-control, rapid heartbeat. Then he would stop the chemical. This test would determine whether my heart could return to normal on its own or stay elevated, at which point a cardiac arrest could occur.

If my heart did not correct itself, I would need a pacemaker and defibrillator installed. Without it, I risked another sudden cardiac arrest if my heartbeat surged too high. The doctor explained it all with such confidence that Connie and I left without asking many questions. The meeting felt like a blur. This was becoming the new normal: schedule a doctor appointment to discuss something major, wait forever, and leave with more confusion than when you started.

The doctor was remarkably busy and highly sought after. My procedure had to be scheduled soon, but so did everyone else's. The receptionist explained they needed to contact my insurance and get the procedure approved. It could take as long as two weeks. Be patient and wait for the scheduler's return call. "Be patient." The story of my life. Can you relate? The rules of the human condition almost always come with patience attached. I had a sense that something was about to happen, but I didn't know what.

CHAPTER 30:
THE THIRD INTERVIEW

By mid-August, I was still waiting for the doctor to confirm my procedure. The days ground on slowly. I decided to stop driving altogether until I knew what was going on with my heart. Another episode like the one that landed me in the hospital would have been catastrophic behind the wheel. Once again, the human condition brought its familiar lessons: patience, confusion, and anxiety.

Then I received an email: the company wanted to meet with me for the third and final interview. I was among five remaining candidates for two positions. The final interview would be at the office an hour away, on Saturday, August 31st, 2024. I was to be there at 7:00 a.m. sharp, dressed in business attire. My future sales manager was thrilled I got the call back but reminded me I was not guaranteed the position—so I needed to bring my best.

I knew I would get this job. I just knew it. Faith had brought me this far; He would not let me down. I gave thanks and rejoiced. My heart soared. Was this really happening? How do I prepare? My friend had advised me simply to be myself and focus on the questions. My mind centered entirely on the interview.

Connie was ecstatic for me. We went out and bought a new suit at the discount store. Corporate attire—it had been 25 years since I last wore a suit and tie for anything other than a funeral. I didn't want to overdo it, so I chose pieces I could mix and match. My spirits lifted, and I looked forward once again to the journey ahead. I had been selling real estate for more than two decades. Would my experience matter?

I couldn't help but think about my age. I would almost certainly be the oldest in the group—20 years older than my interviewers the first time around. By the time I had hitchhiked to the Grand Tetons to climb, they were just starting to walk. It gave me a moment of pause and reflection. I was learning to accept my human condition with grace, not by choice but by force. God had placed me in a place of new beginnings. From the day I lay in the street without a heartbeat to now, my life had become a whole new saga.

Life has a way of aging you on the outside. Yet I can still remember my younger self on the inside. When you look in the mirror, do you see your older self? Can you still catch a glimpse of that younger version of you? I remember when life was full of new beginnings—and that feeling was starting to return to me. The human condition we experience can sometimes feel like a raging thunderstorm, blowing in quickly and leaving just as fast. The storm's damage remains, but the sun shines again, and a beautiful rainbow appears.

I felt that way often. Life had handed me death to confront. I had never lost sight of that video playing in my mind—the blue people below as I perched on that pole, forever etched in my mind's eye. The wall of magnificent light that engulfed me at times reminded me of my human condition. I am sure that, as you read my account of life's roller coaster ride, you may very well be sitting behind me, feeling the same twists and turns. My purpose is to tell you to listen—to hear God and the Holy Spirit speaking softly in your heart.

It may not seem obvious at the time, but it is there, gently reminding you that His hand is on you. Take hold of it, and cling tightly to His promise. He wants us to be happier than we could possibly imagine. He made us pure and perfect in His image. The human condition that we meander through is life itself. And it is free will that brings us to Him and His grace. He has granted me His grace and mercy so many times that I simply begin each conversation with Him rejoicing and giving thanks. You can do the same. No matter what surrounds you, His light is pure. It erases all darkness.

As I was beaming with excitement, I had overlooked one thing—my procedure had yet to be scheduled. One thing the doctor did make clear was that having a pacemaker placed in me was no small matter. I would be restricted for a substantial period. The device would be slipped under the skin, and electrical leads would be attached to areas of my heart. That site would need time to heal. Being too active was out of the question.

Finally, I received a call from the doctor's office. I had been waiting next to the phone for weeks. The scheduler told me that my insurance had approved the procedure, and I was scheduled for the second week of October. Bells and whistles went off in my head. My friend reminded me that if I got the job, I would have to fly to Houston, Texas, for a week of mandatory orientation. The entire group of newly hired sales associates would be involved in long, daily training. They called it "The Mountain."

I didn't even know if I had the job yet. I was about to undergo a procedure that could end with a pacemaker and at least a few weeks of downtime. *Dear God, what is the plan now?* I went into that old, familiar place of stress and anxiety. I tried to explain to Connie the difficulty of the convergence of the two timeframes.

If I had the pacemaker surgery, I might very well lose the job opportunity. How could I choose between health—and very likely life—and the much-needed, essential job opportunity? I called my potential sales manager to see if I could reschedule the third interview. That was a definite no-go.

I called the doctor's office and tried to get the scheduler on the phone. She didn't call back for a week. I explained the condensed version of this story to the poor woman, and she said she would see what she could do. She would talk to the doctor and explain the timing conflict. Was there anything he could do? Later that day, I received a call. The doctor agreed to do the procedure on Friday, August 30th, at 6:00 p.m. He would perform one more procedure before me—I was to be the last person in line.

A room was set aside for me in case a pacemaker needed to be implanted in my chest. If that happened, the third interview scheduled for 7 a.m. the next morning would be off. Did I buy a suit for nothing? Was this all just another exercise in futile patience? I prayed for guidance and left the entire situation up to Him.

Friday came, and I was preparing for the procedure. I called my friend to explain the situation—there was a possibility I might not make it after all.

I was prepped and ready. As I lay there waiting to be sent back, Connie held my hand. I felt her love and compassion. I was so blessed to have her with me through the entire ride. I never could have managed without her. God had blessed me 31 years earlier with a wife who would be with me no matter what.

I was sent back to the operating room, where the familiar team stood around in their surgical gowns and gloves. Everything was straight down to business. The doctor came in and spoke to his staff. The anesthesiologist was ready to give me the familiar twilight medicine. They inserted a catheter into my femoral artery. I felt the sting as it was sent up through the main artery, followed by the hot sensation of the dye and anesthesia.

I had no sense of time. I vaguely recalled the doctor talking to the nurse, and then my heart felt like it was coming out of my chest. Panic set in. What was that? Something very real was happening, but what was it? What seemed like minutes felt much longer. Then I heard the doctor say, "We're all finished."

I went to sleep and woke up in the recovery room. Connie was there with me. She leaned over and said my heart had passed the test. They had tried to induce an out-of-control heartbeat, but my heart had compensated and returned to normal when the chemical stress was stopped. I did not need a pacemaker. The doctor simply placed a loop recorder inside me to read and assess my heart rate via a Bluetooth device.

The doctor came in to visit for a minute or two. He said my heartbeat was normal and that my heart was working very well, considering what it had been through. He admitted that he fully expected to have to place a device inside of me, and he was genuinely delighted with the outcome.

I told him about my job interview scheduled for the next morning. Did I have to stay overnight? No—I was free to go. I just needed to be careful of the site where he had entered my artery. Because I was on blood thinners, that was his only concern.

I prayed with tears in my eyes. God had been in the room with me the entire time. He showed Himself to me that night. I had placed every ounce of faith in Him, and He delivered on His promise—once again. I promise this to you: trust in Him just once, and put your entire faith in His plans for you. His will be done.

I hopped off the bed, and my wife helped me get dressed. I did have a couple of major wounds, but that didn't faze me. I was out of there.

It was 10:30 p.m. by the time we arrived home. I had to eat something, as I hadn't been allowed to eat all day. I was in bed and asleep almost instantly. I had to leave no later than 5:45 a.m. to make it to my interview by 7:00 a.m. Early to rise and greet the day with everything I could assemble of my old self.

I arrived slightly early and met the four other gentlemen who were in line for the same job I was applying for. I was twice their age, with ten times their experience—and I knew it. I am a leader. I am smart. I know who the buyer is. I have written a complete manual on how to help people achieve homeownership.

I was the last one called in. The people in the room were my friend, the Regional Vice President of Sales, and the Vice President of Operations. They were friendly and welcoming. I sat down in front of the VP of Sales. He asked a few basic questions, and I framed my answers around the résumé he had in front of him. I had sold over 500 homes. I specialized in the first-time homebuyer. I taught all phases of real estate and mentored dozens of agents to success.

Then the awkward question came up: "How many houses did you sell in the last two years?"

I answered, "Three."

The raised eyebrow told me I was headed into dark territory. He asked why I had sold so few, given my impressive résumé. I felt my heartbeat and replied, "I died."

The look on his face told me everything: *all in, or go home.*

I started by telling him about my hockey background. I had done my research on everyone in the room. I mentioned that he was from South Dakota and had been a hockey player and referee. I told him I, too, had played high-level hockey. I also shared that I had played in Omaha, Nebraska—where the VP of Operations sitting behind me had started his construction career. The looks on both of their faces told me it was time to take charge of the room.

I had been in situations like this many times before. I had been interviewed by police chiefs, majors, generals, school principals, and CEOs of major corporations. Now it was my time to shine. I had arrived the day after yet another miracle, and I had my angels in the room.

I told them I was one simple Google search away. They could read all about me and the one-percent club I belonged to. I made sure they understood that I was special—and confident.

I didn't want to take up the entire time with all the details, so I told them they would have to read the book when I was finished. Nonetheless, I left everyone with their jaws open and amazed. The VP of Operations remarked that I was clearly a warrior. "Yes," I said, "I was a warrior in more ways than one." I had spent the previous evening on an operating table for the final test of my heart. I was healthy and had defied the odds once again.

The interview concluded with their standard, "Do you have any questions for us?" I had several, but I didn't want to appear uninformed. One I did ask was about the company itself: "Why should I want to work for you?" It might have seemed bold, but I am a firm believer in Stephen Covey's habit #4: think win-win, or no deal. This has always been my standard with anyone I conduct business with.

The VP of Sales said it was because of their Core Values, which were to be publicly stated every time a future homeowner was spoken to. He rattled them off in a memorized fashion. Something felt a little canned, but I was happy to hear someone speak about core values. I am a man who puts his faith in God 100%. I do not—and will not—waiver on that core value. He shook his head in affirmation and thanked me for coming in. They would be in touch.

I thanked them and left. On the way home, I felt good about my presentation. I didn't have the job definitively, but I felt confident. The ride home was filled with prayers of rejoicing and thankfulness. For now, this felt like the right step for my comeback. With so many miracles and prayers answered, this at least felt like the right start.

I received a call the following Thursday, inviting me to come back on Saturday. They wanted to conduct an active day of learning and sales training to see how I would perform. I was excited and agreed immediately. I was reminded that one of the job requirements was to drive a car no more than five years old by the end of December if I was fully hired.

Connie and I shared our only car; it was seven years old and had been driven hard over the past two and a half years by her food delivery work. It would have to hold out until I could get a paycheck or two.

I woke up early on Saturday and put on my best clothes. A tie wasn't required, but I wore one anyway. I had to be at the office by 8:00 a.m. sharp and could not be late.

I left in plenty of time, grateful for the opportunity. The trip to the office was an hour long, and I took the highway that ran along the Gila Indian Reservation. It was the fastest route with the fewest stops.

About forty-five minutes from my destination, I pulled onto the 65 MPH highway. I was following a food truck doing 45 MPH. Oh no—impossible to pass on the two-lane road. My impatience rose with every minute. I lost my sense of peace.

Then I saw a brief spot to pass. I pulled out, stepped on the gas, accelerated to around 70 MPH, and cleared the truck just before oncoming traffic rounded the bend. As I finished passing, my car shut off. The radio was still on, but nothing else worked. The steering was stiff, the gas pedal useless. A warning light appeared on the dashboard. I found a place to pull over by a construction site.

I lifted the hood in my dress clothes. There was a faint smell of smoke from the engine. The oil was new. The battery was new. The supercharger had just been replaced. Nothing happened when I tried to restart it. A kind man from the construction site helped me attempt a jump start. Smoke, nothing else. My car was dead on the way to the final requirement for the job. The human condition had shown up again.

I immediately called Connie. She got out of bed and drove over with my daughter's car. I would be only fifteen minutes late. They understood that these things happen. I assured them I now had reliable transportation and that it would never be a problem again. Not exactly the ideal way to start the day, but I arrived flustered and ready. I had to put my best foot forward and act like nothing had gone wrong.

Has this ever happened to you? Just when life starts to improve, your own human condition shows up to ruin the day? What do you do? When life punches you in the face, it's time to listen to the man in your corner cheering you on. I hear that voice and get up swinging, like the movie *Rocky*. Beaten, battered, barely able to see—I dig in and hear His voice: "Get up and fight the devil! You can do it; I am right here with you!"

I have come to completely understand the nature of the human condition. It creates a choice: trust God, or trust myself. I simply chose to have faith in my Creator. I am not remotely capable of navigating life's unknowns without the map He has written. He wants us to be happy, so we must choose happiness. He wants us fulfilled; without His love, we will always be left wanting. I chose Him.

CHAPTER 31:
WELCOME ABOARD: DO AS I SAY, NOT AS I DO

I arrived that Saturday still flustered. I performed very well in training. Most of it was orientation on the sales process. This company relied heavily on a 48-page manual to be memorized word for word. The script allowed zero deviation. I had to conduct it exactly as written before being allowed to sell anything.

The first step in the process was a trip to Houston, Texas. We stayed in a nice executive hotel, and we were paid $500 to cover expenses. The entire trip was covered, so I only needed to worry about baggage. The food was excellent. We spent eight hours a day listening to talks from the CEO and President. Everything I heard about the Core Values resonated with me. The financial prospects were phenomenal. Many of the salespeople were making well into six figures.

They promised a steady stream of 500 qualified leads. I only had to close 18 sales a year to meet their standard and keep my job. The benefits were a first for me as I had never had any form of insurance or retirement. Everything sounded like God had placed me in the right place at the right time. We had the opportunity to visit headquarters and see every phase of the business. They were transparent and profitable.

I started memorizing my script immediately. I even had part of it memorized on the first day—well ahead of the rest of the group. I was on cloud nine. I couldn't wait to dive into my new role. I had all the skills the others in the room lacked. I was the oldest person, with the most hands-on experience with the exact type of client they were spending millions to attract. My heart was soaring. The Core Value speech had me from the very beginning. It was a moving moment.

Something seemed a little off from the beginning. I have always been good at making it to the finish line, and after what I had just experienced, it felt like I was going to have a head start on this new success. But a nagging gut reaction lingered. Everything felt fake, staged, full of production clichés. Nonetheless, I was employed and thankful for the positive step forward.

Once home, I had a day off before training in the sales process began. This process was strictly by the book. No room for deviation. That was okay with me, I liked things that were easy to follow. I had been using my own version of the same process for decades. How hard could it be to learn a new one?

The group I was training with was fairly concerned with memorization. The volume was considerable, requiring constant effort to master the process. I have always excelled at memorization, so I just dug in and did the work. I quickly mastered the routine. I finished the training early and, within three weeks, was tested out. I was allowed to start making calls and taking leads.

If you have ever been in sales, you know about hot leads. These are the people who call you, eager to know how to buy or use your product. Hot leads require a management system for follow-up. Then there are cool leads: well-meaning, but often not qualified to afford or use your product or service. These leads are stored in a drip system, touched periodically to see if they will produce fruit in the future. Finally, there are extremely cold leads—people who cannot use, afford, or need your product at all. These are discarded quickly.

What wasn't adding up was the same question each lead would ask: "How much is the rent?" or "How do I rent to own?" The guaranteed leads promised at the Houston orientation—the ones from "The Mountain"— were supposed to come from a qualified source. These prospects were meant to be genuinely interested in buying a home, making sales almost guaranteed for anyone following the process.

Instead, we soon discovered that the prospects were from a city three hours away, looking for brand-new homes for less than $1,350 per month with zero downpayment and no closing costs. What nobody said aloud was that these potential buyers had been captured with very misleading advertising. So much for the Core Value speech.

I started the job on the first day of November. In the five months I worked there, I managed to sell four properties in one month, putting me at number one in national sales. The drive was becoming hard and often dangerous. I was commuting late after ten-hour workdays. Locals drove recklessly, and I had witnessed several serious accidents.

I knew I was at the end of the road with this job. The Core Values were a complete lie. Nothing about the company honored the values I thought we shared. It was all a packaged bill of goods, designed to convince prospects of a value that didn't exist.

Connie saw how hard I worked. She completely supported me when I came home late and exhausted, only to get up early and do it all over again. My health was sometimes an issue. I kept track of my heart rate, and often at work it would spike over 170 BPM.

The call from my cardiologist really got my attention. They requested an immediate appointment to review the readings from the loop recorder implanted at the end of August. Usually, I was the one calling them, not the other way around. The appointment was set for early the next morning, leaving me a night to worry about what might come next.

I arrived early, needing to be at work an hour away by 9:00 a.m. The technician showed me to the examination room, and I waited. Connie wasn't with me since it was a workday. The doctor came in, happy as always, and glad to see me. He had a file in hand, sat down, and asked how I was feeling. I told him I was working very long hours in the job I had interviewed for the last time we met at the hospital.

He asked if I was exercising. I told him Connie and I had joined a gym and were using a trainer two to three times a week. Then he spoke about the sudden call and appointment. The loop recorder in my chest had been picking up regular spikes in my heart rate. He showed me the readout: at least once a day, my heart rate spiked as high as 190 BPM, then returned to normal immediately.

I pulled out my phone and compared it to the app I used with my watch. Sure enough, each spike coincided with the app. The only difference was my numbers were about 30 points lower than the device in my chest. That got my attention. What I thought was 145 BPM was actually far closer to the limit of my heart's capacity. And it happened right in the middle of my workday, often on days filled with calls and busywork.

I had been privileged to work with amazing leaders in the past. The man leading me now was not among them. I was keenly aware of the stress this caused. My life was devoted to faith in God and the people I surrounded myself with. He was not the person I was going to retire with.

How many of you have been in the exact same place? Stuck in a toxic environment, trapped by the job itself, stuck in the mud of the mundane. Miserable. I was.

It was one of the hardest things I had ever stuck with. I kept telling myself that if I could just make it a year, I would prove something to myself. If I could make it a year, I would get through the difficult stage of realizing just how hard it would be to find qualified prospects among the flood of bad leads.

The day they told me they had sold virtually every home to an investor who would rent them out, I was done. I called in sick the next day. I was going to fire my boss. My plan: return to the open real estate market. I had been successful in the past, and I felt I had earned a new set of spurs working in the conditions I was about to leave. The market was just as hard being self-employed, minus the shenanigans.

I called a close friend with great connections and met her for coffee. She immediately put me in touch with a broker who was delighted to have me come visit.

The next morning, I left with a prayer in my heart and a resignation letter in my hand. My heart spoke to God: *"Dear Lord, a miracle of faith placed me in this position. Here I am, moving in another direction, away from all the toxicity. Please send me a sign that this is Your will and not mine."*

As I drove on the highway, remembering several close calls from drunk drivers and speeding semi-trucks, my mind focused on the next conversation I was about to have with my friend and the sales manager.

He had believed in me from the beginning. I felt a profound sense of disappointment that I had let him down. It would not make him look good that his recommended hire quit after six months. He was just as frustrated as I was, but he felt compelled to continue. I had seen my heart rate rise to dangerous levels from the stress of the job. I simply wasn't wired to lower my standards. I worked on faith, and I felt a type of darkness here that was hard to explain.

CHAPTER 32:
HERE'S YOUR SIGN

I was approaching a tiny town, just before I was to turn off at the office. Once again, I focused on a prayer for clarity, lost in my thoughts. Suddenly—BANG! A small car was traveling toward me at about 80 MPH. An old farmer in a pickup truck I was following pulled in front of the oncoming car. The young driver never touched the brakes. He hit the broadside of the truck, sending it spinning into the air. The car's front end exploded upward and veered into an irrigation ditch. Tools from the truck's bed flew everywhere. I was about twenty feet from the collision.

I grabbed my phone and called 911. I jumped out and ran to the truck first. The farmer, in his seventies, was dazed but otherwise unharmed. I ran across the debris to the ditch, where the car lay on its side. The front was missing and steaming. The driver was conscious but struggling. His left arm hung out the window with a severe compound fracture above the wrist.

The farmer joined me as I tried to calm the driver. I had seen severe injuries before and had some emergency training. The fracture was pumping blood quickly, he had severed an artery, and the bleeding needed to stop. I asked the farmer for his skinny belt to use as a tourniquet. He also had a long screwdriver in a side holster, which I used to twist the belt tight enough to pinch off the damaged artery.

The bleeding stopped, but his bone was badly mangled. I worried he might tear the artery completely. The driver screamed in pain and complained of severe abdominal pain. I felt his stomach, it was hard. I feared internal injuries. I thought of Dale Earnhardt, the stock car driver who died in a crash from sudden deceleration. An object in motion remains in motion unless acted upon by an outside force. His organs had suffered the same violent stop from 80 MPH. He was in serious trouble.

I heard the faint sound of sirens. *"Dear God, have mercy on this young man."* I prayed for angels of mercy to surround him. We were still in a rural area. The closest fire department and rescue units were ten miles away.

The sheriff's department arrived first. I held the belt tightly around his arm and yelled for a tourniquet. A deputy retrieved a medical bag from her car, navigated the ditch bank, and applied a proper tourniquet while I held my makeshift device. The fire department's sirens grew closer.

I explained to the sheriff what had happened and highlighted the young man's abdomen, suspecting internal injuries. He was in his early twenties and beginning to show signs of shock. At first combative, he was now glazing over and breathing shallowly. I prayed again for the emergency responders to arrive quickly.

Several more sheriff units arrived and blocked off traffic. The crash site covered the entire highway. I stayed with the young man, encouraging him to remain calm and breathe. He was terrified and in severe pain. I was initially concerned there might be a fire. He would need to be extracted from the vehicle, which was folded up and missing its front end.

I had just experienced God's message in response to my prayer for clarity. Connie's biggest fear had been that highway, and she was right. God had just delivered a full-fledged demonstration of why.

I texted my boss and said I was assisting with an accident and would be arriving late. As all the emergency personnel arrived, my mind drifted back to the reason I was on the road: I was driving to hand in my resignation. I was shaking as I returned to my car. A damaged piece of metal from the accident rested on my hood, far too close for comfort. I closed my eyes and offered a very emotional prayer of thanks. I rejoiced in God's timing once again. I had asked for a sign of clarity and He delivered. It was another miracle. I could have been just ten yards closer and caught in a catastrophic accident.

The resignation was clearly part of the purpose of my journey. I took a few minutes to calm myself and just praise Jesus. Miracles happen every day. I was proof of that. God had also placed me in the right spot for the young man. He would have bled out before help arrived. Later, the sheriff confirmed the young man had internal injuries but had made it to the hospital. I had saved his life that morning. Praise God.

I arrived at the office. My friend and boss said he had seen a post of the accident on social media, with me in the picture holding the young man's arm. I briefly described what had happened. He saw the look in my eyes and asked if I was okay. I handed him the resignation letter I had written, detailing the awful conditions the vice president of sales had created. He agreed with my assessment. I knew the letter might have serious consequences for the VP, but I left it up to him to share it with corporate headquarters.

Failure of leadership was a firing offense, both written in the manual and posted on the wall. If I failed, my manager failed and was to be replaced. My letter exonerated him while highlighting the failures of his boss. Either way, I was disappointed that the core values I had once believed in were missing.

On the way home, I received a phone call from the vice president of sales. As expected, he tried to deflect and avoid responsibility. I simply don't argue anymore. I have learned that toxic people can stew in their own misery without my participation.

I had taken a leap of faith and entered the high-end luxury market with a wonderful Christian man running a genuinely nice office. The environment was comfortable. The office manager was one of the sweetest people I had ever worked with. I spent a lot of time in an office right in the middle of a mall in an exclusive part of town. The clientele was a welcome change from the first-time buyers I had just left. Most of the homes for sale were in the millions. I had sold those types of houses before, but the market had been slow.

I settled into homes in the mid-five-hundred-thousand-dollar range and found immediate success. On my second open house, I met a young man and closed on his home three weeks later. This was the kind of work I had been accustomed to before my accident. I was truly returning to myself. Financially, it was just a matter of time if I kept up this pace. I was much happier. I found time for Connie and my grandchildren. Connie and I were spending real quality time together.

The revelation for me was clear: God had given me the opportunity to stand back up on my own two feet. I could trust my instincts once again, guided by His hand. I had lost myself, but through His mercy and grace, I could see my purpose clearly. He wanted me to succeed. Initially, I had been confused about why a miracle during my procedure led to an alternate ending for my career path. Now, I see it through an entirely new lens.

I have placed my entire existence in the hands of Jesus. Some people believe in coincidence. I do not. One unusual event might be coincidence—but an entire stream of perfectly timed, extremely unlikely intersections? Never. How can someone who sits in darkness dispute the light, no matter how faint it may be to them? It is simply by choice that their own human condition blinds them to the truth. Yet your human condition has one profound benefit: it allows you to see the contrast between light and darkness. All that is necessary is to notice it for the value it represents—the absence of light, and how it makes the light shine all the brighter.

CHAPTER 33:
MY HOPE FOR YOU

I have shared my story over a hundred thousand times. Often, people ask me if I am afraid to die. I have been given the gift of knowing what happens when I am about to transition to the afterlife. It is pure, majestic peace. Do I look forward to returning there? Every day, I accept that it is not yet my time. So, I wait, and I pray for guidance along the way.

As I share my story and listen to those who hear it, a common thread emerges: more questions than answers on the surface. Yet there is power in the experience I have lived. As I convey it, people are often quietly compelled to question their own lives and the choices they make.

When I talk about free will and the human condition, the question often arises: *What if he's right?* The fact is, I have several indisputable experiences that challenge even the most skeptical mind. I welcome that challenge. Humans are equipped with an extraordinary gift: reason and logic. Use it. Test it. Come to your own conclusions. I hope that even a small portion of my experience can help you in your own journey of discovery.

Our intuitive nature drives us down countless paths. It is how we are wired: to question, to explore, to learn. Life presents us with perceptions and facts, and we try to make sense of them. Free will allows us to move forward believing in our hypotheses, shaping our own understanding of the world.

Throughout human history, we have relied on trial and error to seek truth. Once we believe we have solved a question, we carry that knowledge with us as a navigational tool. Confirmation bias becomes part of our path—it guides us, strengthens us, and sometimes challenges us.

In short, once we convince ourselves of a truth, we hold it tightly. That commitment gives us the spirit to move forward. When I first awoke in the hospital after my cardiac arrest, I was overwhelmed with questions. I still have questions today, but I carry on.

The schism between God and science often appears vast and opposing. I simply disagree. I believe that understanding God and His infinitesimal design is so far beyond the reach of the human mind that we are constantly trying to disprove what we cannot fully comprehend. We discover laws of physics, and then we use those laws to construct our understanding of the world.

My ability to describe—clearly, in full color and three-dimensional detail—the events that occurred while I lay clinically dead is something I still struggle to understand. How was it possible that the many simple facts I observed were later confirmed without dispute? The white envelope containing the IO tubes used for the IV in my bone marrow. I was clearly gone, and the final attempts to bring me back were already underway.

How was it possible for me to accurately describe the positioning of the police cars and the crowd watching from across the street when I was on the ground, covered by people? Wouldn't I have been terrified if I were actually cognizant—just not breathing and without a heartbeat? The ambulance, M252, was from another fire station, not the engine company across the street. I described the blue shirt the man was wearing the day he pulled me from the car. Clearly, I was present in some other form. I wasn't afraid, only calm and at peace.

How did his wife instinctively know that his presence was a miracle, even though it would not become apparent until nine months later?

Was this a simple coincidence, or a series of events carefully strung together, one by one, by design? Someone once asked me if I believe in angels. Absolutely. Was it an angel who tapped the girl named Angel on the shoulder, urging her to investigate while others were honking for her to drive around me? Did an angel intervene with the man who had traveled Higley Road countless times, yet on this day found himself on the wrong side of the road for reasons he himself could not explain? Was it a coincidence that Valentine was the last name of the paramedic on Valentine's Day?

How did my car get put into park? Sitting there with only my foot on the brake would have been disastrous. Why did it happen at that intersection and not at home, where I was fully focused on going? Was it because Connie wasn't there? She would have arrived home to find her husband dead, with no one present to help or call 911.

What were the chances that a police officer was in the adjacent neighborhood? I have been told I was mere seconds away from certain death or catastrophic brain injury. And how much of a coincidence was it that I had written an influential letter to the mayor about the lack of AED technology in every patrol car; at the very time the police department had been fighting for those devices for over a year?

Consider the number of outcomes—uncanny, precise, and life-preserving—that aligned for my survival.

I began by discussing the human condition. We all live day by day, bobbing and weaving through the stream of life. In our attempts to be more today than we were yesterday, have we forgotten what is most important to us? Pick up that crystal ball again. Take a deep, long look. Peer into the depths of your future. What do you see? Can you see yourself at the very end of your life, buried deep within the crystal? Can you see the reel of your own existence playing before you?

My hope is to meet each one of you somehow. I want to sit with you and listen to your life story. Maybe we can meet on a social media page. Possibly, as I continue to speak, you will attend an event and come to me afterward to share your story. My purpose has evolved into a deep caring for the individual nature of your life. Somehow, mine was spared. It's time for me to give it back to you.

As I continue to navigate my life on the path laid before me, the nature of the world will not change. I can only affect my surroundings, the people I surround myself with, and how I relate to them. I have free will, just as you do. Living with the video of that Valentine's Day constantly playing in the front of my mind's eye leaves me with a reminder of what could have been.

I can now say that I have looked into the crystal ball of my life and seen many scenes I wish I could change. Many times, I am overcome with regret and sadness for what might have been. If I had just done or said one thing differently, what would be different now? I know I will someday return to the peace of that light. I have the end in mind very clearly now. My life—and what I do with it—is what will fill the rest of the time until then.

My hope is for you to know there is something more after our bodies fail and we cease to exist in this place in the universe called Earth. The potential you have is so great. Look deep into the crystal. How many lives can you touch and help through the understanding of the human condition you see within your own soul? There is so much more than living day to day, simply trying to make it better than yesterday.

We can build and live in a place where, no matter what occurs, there is always hope for tomorrow. When I say I rejoice in everything, it places me in a frame of faith in the good that is yet to come. I look for it with anticipation. The time we have to live our lives is finite. None of us know the true expiration date of our existence. I have been blessed with a second chance. Every day, I give thanks for the new day and a beating heart—literally.

The heart in my chest is damaged, and I know it. The time I have left is finite. I am called to live my life with purpose now. I want to spread the word as best I can. I hope to live like tomorrow may never come, and so should you. I have learned, with deep understanding, that I am fragile. Life is fragile. You are fragile. So, make something of it. Look into yourself so you can see outside of yourself. Who you touch in life matters. Each time you touch another human being, do your best to make them better. You will become better yourself for doing so.

Wake up and ask yourself: *who is going to be your next miracle?* What can

I do today to increase the value of the person who crosses my path? My story of survival and miracle has been a source of hope for many people I meet. The simple act of sharing an amazing story often creates a reaction of hope in their own condition. They begin to share their story, and it becomes my opportunity to listen.

When you become aware of another human being and the weight of their own condition, it enhances your own in the most positive way. By listening to another, you learn about yourself. Creating a bond with a stranger is extremely satisfying. Feel their pain and discover your own. Identifying with their struggle shapes the way you handle yours. My hope for you is to foster hope in others.

This manifestation of the best in others becomes the path to the best in yourself. What a wonderful feeling it is to see someone light up in the middle of a dark moment you never knew they were having. When a stranger shows compassion for a hurting soul, the healing that takes place is almost magical. How many times have we passed by someone in the grocery store without so much as a smile or hello? Start today and find out for yourself. The glow you will see in that person is amazing. A random compliment to a random person can soften even the most hardened soul.

Consider the impact it must have had on my lifesavers. I visited them one by one. They mattered to me, and they knew it. The paramedic who made the decision to give me the adjusted shock that saved my life was in tears when we first met. She was stunned to see me standing there, alive and ready for a hug. Before I left, she shared a deep human emotion—gratitude.

She explained that she had been a paramedic for only a few years. She spoke of the difficulty of watching people die and wondering what their lives might have become if they had lived. She described the pain of treating patients whose choices cost them their lives, or the lives of others. She was newly married and had found love. Through sobs, she told me how grateful she was and then shared a story.

Early in her career, still a rookie, they received a call about an unconscious man. His girlfriend had come home to find him on the floor from an apparent drug overdose. He had no heartbeat and was not breathing. She was hysterical and attempting CPR. The paramedic went into the protocol she had been trained for. After repeated shocks from the AED, he sputtered back to life.

I told her that experience must have been traumatic. She said it was her first code and that she had revived him. I sensed something deeper and asked if he made it. She began to sob again and said that he had. I congratulated her. Then she wiped her eyes and told me they were called back a week later. He had overdosed again. This time, it was too late. She felt a profound sense of failure. It nearly broke her, and she considered quitting.

What a tragedy, to do everything right and still lose. He did not survive his own human condition. He never saw the miracle of life given back to him through her heroic effort. How hopeless that must have felt. She smiled, hugged me tightly, and before I left said, "I got my hope back because you wanted to live." I will never forget that moment. My life mattered to her. I had just experienced the power of purpose through another's human condition.

If you have ever performed CPR, you know the face of that person never leaves you. No matter how many times you've done it, something small can bring it all back. The human whose ribs you break bonds with your psyche. What a profound experience it is to push life back into someone with your own hands. You are tired, sore, aging—but you press on. Their life depends on it.

What a connection that creates. When do you stop? What is going through your mind? I taught CPR for many years. I never imagined I would one day be the recipient. The only time I performed CPR, my sole thought was to pace myself. Don't get tired. The elderly man's life depended on it. I intended for him to survive. I remember his gray face and the sound of his ribs cracking. His life mattered to me. I refused to give up.

I share this because there was a deep connection between those who were there at the beginning, when time was critical. Each responder formed a bond with a total stranger. When I returned later, the raw emotion they showed reflected their commitment to my life. What a gift it is to know that

I lived. How many lives will you touch with just a smile or a random compliment?

The twenty minutes or so that I was not here placed me in a unique position with caregivers. Often, I am asked the quiet question, "What was it like?" I replay my experience as best I can. It makes me wonder why they ask. Some are curious. Others are spiritual and seeking reassurance. Often, they have lost someone they love and simply want to know—were they okay?

Every weekend, while working open houses, conversations inevitably turn to life. I don't sell houses, I build relationships. Eventually, Valentine's Day 2022 comes up. "You're that widow maker guy—I saw you on TV." What a gift it is to have a warm conversation about dying. People stay and talk about family, work, and what brought them there. This is the serendipity my purpose has created. I have found joy in the hearts of strangers. What a privilege it is to learn from others.

My hope for you is that you, too, find opportunities to stop, listen, and learn through others. It is deeply fulfilling. I have taken a series of difficult calamities and turned them into opportunity. When I meet someone new, I look into their eyes. I see light—it comes from within. As I share my life and its vulnerabilities, I look forward to the day we meet and you share yours with me.

Ultimately, I have come to understand the meaning of the miracle I was given. Faith is an action word. In moments of loss, pain, or exhaustion, I looked upward and found discernment I could trust. My life has been a gift. I encourage you to take my truth and make it your own. There is more to your existence than you realize. Each of us carries a gift meant to be shared. Miracles like mine happen every day. Be someone's miracle today.

CHAPTER 34:
YOUR TOMORROW HAS JUST BEGUN

Let's begin today by thinking about tomorrow. Given the finite time we have here together, I want to guide you toward what tomorrow could look like as you step into your today. Consider the power of starting each morning the way I do, give thanks for the new day and your own beating heart. I can say with complete honesty: I am thankful to wake up every day.

Before I even glance at the time, I seek the grace of God. I ask that each day be filled with opportunities to meet someone who may desperately need a miracle. I want to be the one who shows up unannounced, the person who becomes their moment to rejoice. Countless moments and chance meetings have crossed my path simply because I am looking for them.

My suggestion for making your tomorrow better today is simple: practice this activity daily. Focus on the person you are and who you want to become. Will you allow your human condition to dictate your outcomes, or will you predict your reaction before your condition shows up? My experience has taught me the most valuable lesson: gratitude. I start each day with total gratitude for being alive.

Gratitude is the beginning of happiness. If I am grateful, I am open to hope. Hope is the solution to your human condition. Without it, you are a slave to circumstance. You will never feel free from the strife and struggles of daily life. But with gratitude, others see the light in you. You begin to see others differently. Empathy turns into understanding. Understanding allows you to perform the most profound action for someone who is hurting.

The ability to truly listen to another person takes conscious effort. Most of us, including me at times, fill the pauses in conversation with our own thoughts instead of hearing what is actually said. That is not listening. That is conversing. If you want to be a miracle for someone, it takes active listening. Stephen Covey calls it habit number five: "Seek first to understand, then to be understood." That is the beginning of truly comprehending what is in another person's heart and mind.

Gratitude serves another purpose: it brings contentment. To be content is exceedingly rare when human condition surrounds us. How can one be content amidst suffering? Where is satisfaction in pain and uncertainty? Yet gratitude creates hope. And hope gives you the strength to move forward. And move forward we must.

By beginning tomorrow, today, you keep your eyes on what is to come, not what has passed. As you gather strength day by day through hope, life begins to change. Your reactions shift, guiding you toward solutions. Think back to the satisfaction of persevering through a challenge. Didn't that experience fortify you for the next battle? I believe it did.

Throughout my life, I have ridden a roller coaster of difficulty and triumph. Each difficulty was an opportunity to grow and learn. Each triumph reinforced my path. I rejoice in all things. I am grateful for both. Each time I face the replay in my mind of the period I was not alive, I am reminded of the miracle of life given to me.

As I wake, I give thanks for what is yet to come. Gratitude happens today; hope is for tomorrow. Every day I meet someone whose heart I can learn from, simply because I am looking for them. How refreshing it is to have faith in the path you walk. Does it change the human conditions around you? No—but when they inevitably arrive, your perspective will be ready for the solution.

Let's look into the crystal ball again. Can you predict how you will respond the next time life wobbles, trying to knock you down? My hope is that you will see the finite nature of your life, how fragile it can be. I am living proof of both fragility and finite existence. There is no warning. You will not know when suddenly you are looking back at your life from above.

Hopefully, you too will be engulfed in the peace of the light I experienced. I know with every fiber of my being that I will arrive there again, without notice. This is what drives my purpose in sharing this story. What an incredible gift I have been given. No matter what happens, I live with complete confidence that this life is short and that what follows has already been foreshadowed. I am deeply grateful for this revelation.

How could I not share it, shout it from the mountaintops? Sitting atop that light pole, watching the world below with complete ambivalence, left me with a profound understanding. I wish I had answers for those who shared the terror of darkness and suffering in their near-death experiences. Many replayed fear and pain in their minds, a stark contrast to the peaceful video that played for me.

Others I have spoken with or read about describe personal hell—clawing on walls, darkness filled with agony. Hearing their stories sends shudders down my spine. The contrast reminds me to revisit my own mind's eye for the comfort of the light, the quiet peace, the overwhelming sense of love I felt.

The horrors they experienced remind me of the moment after I was revived. I was lost in the darkness of my mind—terrified, yet alive. The darkness was physical, not spiritual. I would not wish upon anyone the nightmares that can accompany being clinically dead. This drives me still. When I wake in the night, I say a prayer of gratitude. I am not immune to the darkness of dreams. But I am immune to the darkness of my day. Because I am grateful and hopeful, I know deep within my soul what will become of me.

Never give up on yourself. Find your gratitude and express it as often as you can. Someone out there needs to hear about your hope. They will be grateful if you step into their life—on purpose or by accident. You will find your strength and share it. Thank you for being you.

I hope your tomorrow has just begun.

ABOUT THE AUTHOR

Kevin Mohatt lives wiith his wife Connie in Gilbert, Arizona, and is a full-time real estate agent serving Phoenix and the Southeast Valley. He is also a public speaker and mentor for Realtors.

After a profound life-after-death experience, Kevin felt a clear calling to share what he was shown. He has since shared his story with tens of thousands of people, guided by a deep belief that this message was entrusted to him for a purpose—and now, he shares it with you.

LETTER FROM THE EDITOR

One of the most curious adaptations of the human species is our ability to forget our own mortality. We chart our course and live day to day disregarding the fact that our time is finite. Pondering our demise might otherwise interrupt our plans, or, send us into a spiral from which we may never recover. In 2020, reeling from my own derailment of sorts, I began to reacquaint myself with God. Being a person of science (a crime scene investigator and later teacher), I struggled with my faith and the hand I had been dealt. I began to investigate God as I investigated crime scenes. I found Him to be wholly other than I realized and in order to deal with that revelation I began writing. After publishing a couple books myself, I began to see miracles all around me. A chance encounter with a modern day Lazarus on a random social media post led to this book.

My one wish for all readers is to consider the miracles in your own lives. To draft your own stories and live boldly, secure in the knowledge that your life has meaning and purpose. And death is not the end, but a brilliant tomorrow.

Amy Jones Neville

Isaiah 60:1